are you listening?
I have something to say in paint and words...

EurOChild

by kids for kids

bradshaw books
cork, ireland

bradshaw books
Tigh Filí Cultural Centre
Festival House
Pope's Quay
Cork
Ireland
+353-21-4215175
www.eurochild.net
© The Authors, 2009

ISBN 978-1-905374-13-7

Oifig an Aire d'Imeasctha
Office of the Minister for Integration

Designed by Anna Barden and Cristina Álvarez González
Cover art by Sarah Healy, Scoil Mhuire Gan Smál, Ballmote, Co Sligo
Robot by Lisa Crowe, Brierfield N.S., Tuam, Co Galway
Fairy by Nicole Griffin-Healy, Scoil Mhuire, Wellington Rd Cork
Flower by Rosa Gannon, Christ King Girls School Cork

Poetry Contents

Art Contents

Foreword

I was very pleased to have been invited once again to write the foreword to this unique anthology of poetry.

This is the 14th year of its publication, a fact which in itself speaks volumes for the commitment of the team at Tigh Filí to this endeavour.

Children's rights form part of the human rights that the European Union and the Member States promote and respect under international and European treaties. Freedom of expression is one of the most important rights and this book is extremely valuable as it provides children from all over Europe with an opportunity of having their voices heard.

The subjects covered in these wonderful poems offer a glimpse of the things which preoccupy, annoy and fascinate children. Life, death, joy and sorrow are part and parcel of children's daily lives. Indeed, one of the most striking features of this work is the extent to which children throughout Europe share the same experiences and insights into issues which concern, or should concern, society as a whole.

It is said that the best poetry has the power of forming, sustaining and delighting us as nothing else can. I invite you, the reader, to open this book at random and be delighted, moved and provoked by the poems.

Minister Micheál Martin

Acknowledgements

As ever I would like to take this opportunity to thank the thousands of young artists and poets who entered for this year's anthology.

With entries reaching over ten thousand the quality of the work was exceptional and I have tried to include as many children as possible within the publication.

Thanks also to all the parents, teachers and arts organisations in Ireland, France, Germany, Spain, Italy, Finland, Serbia, Czech Republic, Romania, Denmark, Lithuania, India, Malta, Palestine and Poland for their continuing support.

This edition would not have been completed without the dedication of the Eurochild team, many thanks to Anna Barden, Christine Álvarez González, Fidelma Maye, Jana Diblikova, Maire Bradshaw, Sophie Carton, Mary Melvin Geoghegan, Leslie Ryan, Louise Brown, Aisling Lyons, James Crummie and Frances Murphy.

Declan Barron
Editor

Parrot by Laura Woods

Seals

Thomas Creamer
Aughnasheelin N.S.
Ballinamore, Co. Leitrim

The cutest animal is the seal
and it eats fish, squid and eels
The seal cubs are the cutest
things in the spring
The cubs are so defenceless
killing them is so senseless.

The Sea

Emma Daly
Crab Lane, N.S., Ballintemple,
Cork

The sea is a horse,
A strong one of course
It gallops with the waves.
So strong, so fierce, so brave.
And when the wind blows
with its mighty force,
The big strong horse
smashes and crashes
amongst the rocks.
Then on calm days in April or May,
The horse lies sleeping
sound on its hay.

Mermaid by Clare Keaveney Jiménez

American Footballer by Hannah Sheehan

No. But

Gavin Fitzgerald
Crab Lane, N.S., Ballintemple, Cork

No I'm not going to clean my room.
No I'm not going to walk the dog.
No I'm not going to feed the cat.
No I'm not going to clean out the shed.
No I'm not going to cut the grass.
But I will do it For money!!

Cranky Mama

Tom Bond
Crab Lane, N.S., Ballintemple, Cork

'Why did you run over her,
She was in the middle of the road
and it was a red light'
'What do you mean you didn't know
You're colour blind,
You're not colour blind'
'Here come the police,
You better take a long look at my face
because I'm not visiting you in prison'
'That's right officer take him away!'

June

Ben Murphy,
Crab Lane, N.S., Ballintemple, Cork

Warm, excited
Clock is ticking
I'm Ready to go
Summer.

Spring!

Sarah Geary
Scoil Mhuire Wellington Rd, Cork

Spring is the time when the flowers
bloom,
The leaves grow back on the trees,
Spring is quite cold but not as cold as
the winter breeze.

Daffodils poke their heads out,
The birds begin to sing,
Bushes begin to blossom again,
The butterflies spread their wings.

Spring is my favourite time of year,
Because everything in the world is filled
with cheer.

Ladybirds' Tea Party by Laura Cronin

I Meant To Do My Homework Today...

Molly O'Shea
Crab Lane, N.S., Ballintemple, Cork

I meant to do my homework today...
But my dog took me on an adventure!,
She pulled me through the forest,
And my bag got caught on a tree.
I couldn't go back to get it,
Cause my dog is stronger than me!

I meant to wear my uniform today...
But my dog took me on an adventure!,
We went to the pond,
She saw a duck,
I tripped over a stone,
And fell in the muck.

I meant to learn my spellings today,
But my dog took me on an adventure!
We went to a farm,
and I broke my arm,
after she pulled me under a tractor.

I meant to go to school today,
But my dog took me on an adventure!
We were on the road,
And then it got dark and wet,
My dog got hit by a car,
And we spent the rest of the day at the vet!

I Don't Want Homework!

James Killoran
Crab Lane, N.S., Ballintemple, Cork

I don't want homework,
I don't have time,
I want to watch T.V. instead,
It's boring,
I forgot my books,
I don't want to do it!
PLEASE!
Why do we even get homework.
What's in it for me?
PRETTY PLEASE!
You know you want to.
Cooooooooommmmmeeeee   ooonnn!
Why not?
What's the point?
Writing one silly sentence won't
get me into Harvard will it?

Fine!

Shoe Fetish

Jayne Groarke,
Scoil Mhuire Wellington Rd, Cork

One day I knocked
on my neighbour's door,
Only to see
many shoes on the floor.

Big ones, small ones,
Glitter and gold,
Thick straps, thin straps,
Fur boots for the cold.

My friend was embarrassed,
you could see from his face,
for his mother Fi
was an absolute disgrace.

'Oh Jayne' said he, 'my mother Fi
owns all these shoes that you can see.'
92 pairs–We lined them all up
We have no room, we're pretty fed up.

Rot

Lasse Thodt
Grundschule an der Bake, Mönkeberg

Rote Käfer
Auf den Blättern
Sie fressen gerne Läuse
Marienkäfer

Ballerina by Nicole Griffin Healy

Poems

Laura Dennehy
Scoil Mhuire Wellington Rd,
Cork

Long poems,
Short poems,
Sad poems,
Happy poems,
Funny poems,
Boring poems,
Rhyming poems,
Any poems!

Poems with a story,
Poems without work,
Poems with a meaning,
Poems with a quirk!

Feelings

Amy Wong
Scoil Mhuire Wellington Rd, Cork

Lonely
I feel lonely when
I first came to Ireland
Without my mum and dad.

Surprise
I feel surprise when its my birthday
My family get me a birthday cake
They turn off the light and I'm scared
They got me a present and cake.

Sorry
I feel sorry when I do something wrong
But my family will be kind to me .

Angry
I feel angry when my cousin's annoying me
And breaks my things and messes my room.

Sad Ballerina by Jayne Groarke

Spring

Clare Keaveney-Jimenez
Scoil Mhuire Wellington Rd, Cork

Spring is soft colours
Yellow, white and light blue.

Spring is the soft music
Of birds singing again.

Spring is the soft sound
Of rain pouring softly on the roof.

Spring is the soft wool,
Of little lambs.

Spring is the start
Of something strong,
But until summer comes
We should just enjoy spring.

Rainbow by Jack Mulcahy

Flowers

Flowers by Marta Torres González

Emer Murphy
Scoil Mhuire Wellington Rd, Cork

Flowers come in pink and blue
Orange green and purple too

Daisies, tulips and daffodils
All appear on windowsills

It is amazing the giant sunflower
From tiny seed to great tower

Flowers I like them all
But the one I love most of all
Is the little snowdrop
Whose little head drops.

Kesä

Olivia Lehmuskallio
Aarnivalkean koulu, Espoo, Finland.

Kesä maistuu suussa jäätelöltä
Kesä tuntuu lempeältä tuulelta iholla
Kesä kuulostaa meren aalloilta

Joidenkin mielestä aurinkorasvan tuoksu on kesä

Joidenkin mielestä hyttysen pisto on kesä.

Mutta oikeasti kesä on se,
että kun syksy saapuu
emme unohda kesää
vaan se säilyy sydämessämme
talven yli

The Race

Holly Lehane
Scoil Mhuire Wellington Rd, Cork

Closer and closer
As I get to the end,
Just one turn
Around that tight bend.

Now I'm finished
With a smile on my face,
As I win again my usual first place.

When people are running
To congratulate me,
I see my family full of glee.

Mum with a smile upon her face,
And Dad running at a very fast pace.
Brother and Sister are trailing along
Delighted the day has finally gone.

My Pony

Holly Slowey
Scoil Mhuire Wellington Rd, Cork

Over the fence and
Through the field.
My pony protects me
Like a shield.

I'm at the next fence
And I'm riding clear,
The last fence is coming very near.

My pony raced
To the finishing line,
With me on his back.
He's galloping fine.

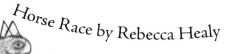

Horse Race by Rebecca Healy

Life

Maha Khurshid
Scoil Mhuire Wellington Rd, Cork

What is life?

Is it real?
Is it a dream?
Is it as rough as a rock?
Is it as smooth as cream?
Do you have fun?
Do you cry a lot?
Do you wonder about it?
Do you not?
Are you smart?
Are you dumb?
Are you caring?
Are you numb?

I think life,
Is really a game,
Each day is a different level,
But never the same.

The Famine

Mia Piccoli
Scoil Mhuire Wellington Rd, Cork

For the poor people who had not even a pound,
Relied on potatoes because they grew from the ground,
All they needed to grow the potatoes was water and a bit of light,
But then came the disease that harmed potatoes,
It was called blight,
No where to turn no help was at hand,
Did they really have to leave their beloved land?
On the coffin ships they left for America,
But for some all that lay before them was death.

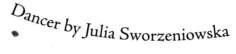

Dancer by Julia Sworzeniowska

My Cat

Vivienne Davis
Scoil Mhuire Wellington Rd, Cork

The scraping of her litter box
her claws against the floor.
She has just done something
nasty need I tell you anymore!

She likes to play with bottle caps
I throw them down the hall
She skids along the marble and
Bounces off the wall!

I love my cat and no one
can change that and that's
a fact!

Shark Dinner by Eavan McLoughlin

Fish

Claire Synnott
Scoil Mhuire Wellington Rd, Cork

Fish are very fishy
I wish I was a fish
I think fish wish do
you think fish wish.

A Fresh Meadow

Laura Froggat
Scoil Mhuire Wellington Rd, Cork

I sit there every day looking out.
People ask me why I do it
I say if you look
you will see.
When they do it all they do is smile and laugh
All I see is a meadow
That's a meadow with fresh blooming flowers.
It's very beautiful can't you see.

My Nan

Alanna Power
Scoil Mhuire Wellington Rd, Cork

My Nan is sweet honey in a jar
Delivered at your door step.
She is Einstein in disguise
A delicate daisy
But don't be fooled!
She is a hard brick.

My Family by Sarah Whelan

Child   Parents   Grandparents

My Mum

Sophie O'Sullivan
Scoil Mhuire Wellington Rd, Cork

She is bright sunshine in the morning
She is a comedy book with no end
She is an encyclopaedia full of information
She is a fizzy drink bubbling all the time
Her heart is as big as the world and she has lots of love to give
Her hugs are teddy bears squeezing me tight
She is a warm oven.

Under a Tree by Clioghna O'Leary

Brandon

Alex Stolz
Scoil Mhuire Wellington Rd, Cork

My brother Brandon...
Is an annoying ucky fly-buzzing in
my ear
But yet a hug
A sweet-tender thing
And then he's the devil
Yelling
And screaming
I just want to shoot him
But I can't
Because he's my brother

33

Note To Self

Sarah O'Leary
Scoil Mhuire Wellington Rd, Cork

All I think about is notes and notes
not shoes, not shirts, not even coats!
My favourite piece is note to self
It's also a book my mom keeps on her shelf
My Mom wakes me up and says time for school
And in there I pass notes from stool to stool
No More Notes! Says the teacher, my Mom and Dad,
So I am left alone and very sad.

In Space

Rebecca Heaphy,
Scoil Mhuire Wellington Rd, Cork

I want to be an astronaut to float
away in space.
I want to walk on the moon like Neil
Amstrong.
I want to watch the planets from inside
a spaceship and look at the earth from above.
I want to see the stars as fireballs up
in space.
I would like to see the ninth planet
and give it its own name.
I would like to call the planet Sirrus, after
an imaginary character I know.
Oh I want to be an astronaut because I
really want to go and float away in space.

Under the Stars by Rachel Moran

Back In Time

Pádraig Connery
Ovens N.S, Co. Cork

If I could travel back in time
To when I heard my first nursery rhyme
I'd find out what I used to like
And take a look at my goldfish Spike.
I'd take a look at all my toys
And monsters that eat little boys
My mum would look under my bed
Where my thoughts would mess with my head

So if I travelled back in time
To when I heard my first nursery rhyme
I'd look at all these brilliant things
And forward to what life brings.

Black

Siobhān Hutchinson
Ovens N.S, Co. Cork

I am the night sky
I am dull, dreary and dark
I don't help people see
I am black.

A Puppy

Eimer Collier
Scoil Mhuire Wellington Rd, Cork

Agit was a puppy
Fickle and full of joy
Anthony was his master
Who laughed all day with joy.

My Pets Are Gone

Saoirse Daly
Scoil Mhuire Wellington Rd, Cork

I had a pet dog
And I had two geckoes
My dog might have been stolen
He might even have run away
And the geckoes ATE each other!

Dog by Julia Balsam

36

Hedgehog Haiku

Adam Lockhart
Ovens N.S, Co. Cork

A little hedgehog
The rustling of prickles
Ouch that really hurts.

Tears by Jack Crowley

The Donkey's Plea

Claire Healy
Ovens N.S, Co. Cork

The humble donkey has always been
the object of laughter and joke.
But really the animal we all know
Is gentle and kindly and meek.

So we all should reconsider
Why we automatically think
That the donkey is completely inferior
And stupidly clumsy and weird.

And why do people always think
That donkeys are really so stubborn
Because If so...
What carried Mary to Bethlehem?

School Nightmares

Hannah O'Sullivan
Ovens N.S, Co. Cork

She walked in
Trembling slightly at the knees
The children were as quiet as
angels so
She said 'Take out your mathsbooks
please'.

That's when all hell broke loose
They were running around pell-mell.
One stood on a table, jumping about
She was horrified when he fell.

'Oh! Me leg! Tis broke!
I'll never play again!
Never play rugby, or football
Like all the other men!'

'Don't be ridiculous!'
The teacher said
'You will play rugby and football
But for now you must rest in bed.'

'Oh Miss, you're wrong!'
Another child shouted
'They'll have to amputate his leg
Sure, I wouldn't doubt it!'

She came back to the class
After calling the child's home
But the sound that met her ears
Made her give a little moan.

It was a horror to her
It made her groan and gasp
The sound that she hated most
The sound of breaking glass.

'Who did it?'
She asked
'Someone has to pay for it.
Now who broke the glass?'

'Twasn't me!'
I was over there!
'Twas too! I saw it!
It was him, I swear!'

'It wasn't him!
It was another boy!'
'Well, which boy was it?'
'Only, joking! Only said it so
you'd get annoyed!'

At my Desk by Emma Mahon

38

'I know who it was, teacher!
I'm not just taking the mickey!
I saw it wit my two eyes,
I tell ya, it was Timmy!'

'Tattletale!' 'Snitch!'
'Wash your mouth out with soap!'
'Would you ever shut your mouth?'
'Ya, you're just a little dope!'

'Children, children!
Please calm down!
You're making such a din-!'
The head came in, on her face,
a frown.

'Teacher I see! You can't
handle this class!
I haven't yet found the teacher
to be desired
But you are fired!'

Her heart went to her head
It pounded, like the slam of a door
Her breath come in rasps
And she fell to the floor.

She woke up sweating
Her sheets, not so clean
But, she was relieved
Because it was just a dream!

TXT!!!!!!

Stephen Kelleher
Ovens N.S, Co. Cork

I wnt dwn ta c my hrse
Coz he woz a bit sik
Nw I av ta cal the vet
And wait 4 nother bill ta colect
O god tis al me money
I Jst 1der iz it wort it all.

Horse by Nicole Griffin Healy

39

Jungle by David Woods

What Is Living?

Aoife O' Shaughnessy
Ovens N.S, Co. Cork

The big white daisies,
The small little bugs,
The slippery worms,
The slimy slugs,

The chirping birds,
The butterfly,
The little ants,
The fox so sly,

The working hands,
The clumping shoes,
We love gardening,
It's what we choose!

Alone In The Undergrowth

Ronan O' Toole
Ovens N.S, Co. Cork

Interest in the badger has been lost over the years,
The black and white wisdom of this big, intelligent old gent
has shown throughout the ages.

He trudges through the undergrowth in his own
slow, unhurried pace
They go in the background and will carry on with these mannerisms...
Until someone notices...
Just as I have.

What Anger Is Like For Me

Carrie Ahern
Ovens N.S, Co. Cork

I hit, shout sometimes fight
I feel frustrated and arrayed
sometimes I feel like giving them
a punch,
But I don't
I keep it in me.
I say some things,
I don't mean.
Then for that I get cross
with myself,
I don't want to be angry
But sometimes I am!

I Said Do Not

Rory Fahy
Ovens N.S, Co. Cork

Do not pick your nose.
Do not play ball in the house.
Do not talk while doing your homework.
Do not talk with food in your mouth.
Do not loose your tie at school.
Do not drool while watching tv.
Do not eat the lead in your pencil.
Do not do this and that.
For heaven sake
Do not read this you're supposed
to be in bed.

The Eyes Have It by Conor Kelleher

41

The Laughing Buddha

The Sun

Lorraine Heslin
Rossan, N.S., Carrigallen, Co. Leitrim

Hannah O' Sullivan
Ovens N.S, Co. Cork

I heard him laugh
As his belly shook
Like a breeze in the wind
The laughing Buddha
Is here somewhere
But where?

Sunlight, helping plants
Under the watch of our eyes
Not unlike a child.

I heard him laugh
It shook the world
Like an earthquake
Such a strong laugh
So strong it would light up a room
So strong it would make someone's day

Sun by Aoife Rogers

Cats

Grāinne Hutchinson
Ovens N.S, Co. Cork

People have lost interest in the cat
Everyone says 'I'm sick of cats I want a dog.'
I think cats are magnificent.
Their glossy fur and the way they cling to you like they really love you.
Their sleek movements and arched backs in the presence of enemies.
The way they linger at your feet when they want a meal
And the way they purr appreciatively at the rub of a back.
Cats bring joy and laughter to the world.
No one could live without cats in their lives!

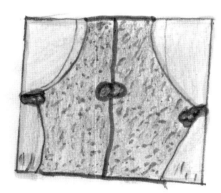

Cat by Yanine Wendez Salvatierra

43

Is This Really Happening

Francie Flynn
Rossan N.S., Carrigallen,
Co. Leitrim

Is this really happening
I think it is
But I don't know I guess it is
Because I see
Her lovely eyes.

She's Nearly There

Alice Holloway
Rossan N.S., Carrigallen, Co. Leitrim

She's nearly there
And the mountain can't tell
Grandfather doesn't know
The world doesn't know
That she's nearly there.
She's on her way
And she's ever so excited.
She's really nearly there.

Girl by Emma de Bhál

What a Ridiculous Idea

Karen Flynn
Rossan N.S., Carrigallen, Co. Leitrim

Mam said, she thought I was silly
To try and eat, talk and sleep upside down.
The eating didn't work out
All I got was stains on my clothes
The talking was easy
Because I'm a chatterbox.
The sleeping was easy
All I did was swap
My head and feet around.

Dreaming by Orla Cahill

No Elbows On The Table Please

Sean Sweeney
Rossan N.S., Carrigallen, Co. Leitrim

Please don't put your elbows on the table
Because its bad manners
Why?
Don't ask me,
Because I don't know
People just told me years and years ago
When I was small.

Standing There Paralysed

Cian McNamee
Rossan, N.S., Carrigallen, Co.
Leitrim

Standing there paralysed
Not moving
I wish the buildings
Could talk or even move
I can't believe
Nothing is happening.

Standing there paralysed
Thinking and thinking
About grass and trees
Birds and goats
There isn't a speck of green
I just can't believe it.

Epitaph For Jack

Rachel Greville
St. Joseph's N.S Co. Westmeath

Here lies a man called Jack,
He fell and broke his back.
There was a loud crack.
That was the end of poor old Jack.

Ghosts by Róisín Mannion

My Epitaph

Aidan Tormey
St. Joseph's N.S Co. Westmeath

There was a man called Aidan.
He listened to Iron Maiden.
He had a wife.
Who stabbed him with a knife.

Epitaph

Amber O'Hanlon
St. Joseph's N.S Co. Westmeath

Here lies a boy called Ted
who didn't realise
he was wearing red
he met a bull,
and now he's dead.
R.I.P.

Guess Who?

Holly Murray
St. Joseph's N.S Co. Westmeath

Cat's prey
Rope tail
Saucer eyes
Vertical body
Tiny brain
Catching pain
Wire chewer
Forked teeth
Sly squeaker!

The Oak Tree On The Hillside

Paul Flaherty
St. Joseph's N.S Co. Westmeath

The devil's trident,
Satan's scary statue,
Demon's afro
Shadow with arms
A silhouetted monster

Mouse by Clare Keaveney Jiménez

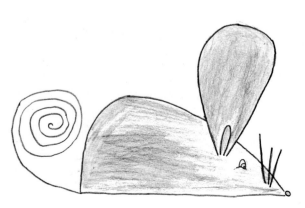

48

Bullies

Nicole Rajendra
Cootehall N.S. Co. Roscommon

Bullies are not nice.
They will stay with you all your life.
They take your things,
And all your treasured rings.

They don't pick on the others.
Because of their gigantic brothers.
They steal your games,
And call you names.
Always ignore them,
You're the one who will end up
getting hurt.

Bullying Is

Emma Ayers
St. Joseph's N.S Co. Westmeath

Staying in a dark room
having no one to talk to
and being called Nasty
names.

Racing Car by Lee Muldoon

49

Brightness Is

Niamh Leech
St. Joseph's N.S Co. Westmeath

Brightness is
a lit up Christmas tree.
Brightness is
A warm fire glazing on a cold dark night
Brightness is
The luminous bloomed daffodils in the green field
Brightness is
The moons reflection on a dark misty night
Brightness is
The flashing lights on a police car
Brightness is
The sun rising in the morning
Brightness is
The lights in the town on Christmas night.

Christmas

Lauri O'Callaghan,
Crab Lane N.S., Ballintemple, Cork

Chilling by the fire
Hearing old tales
Remembering others in prayer
Interesting but still
Singing is my favourite
The tree is shining bright
Merry Christmas to all
And to all a good night
Sleep tight.

Snowman by Ian Leavy

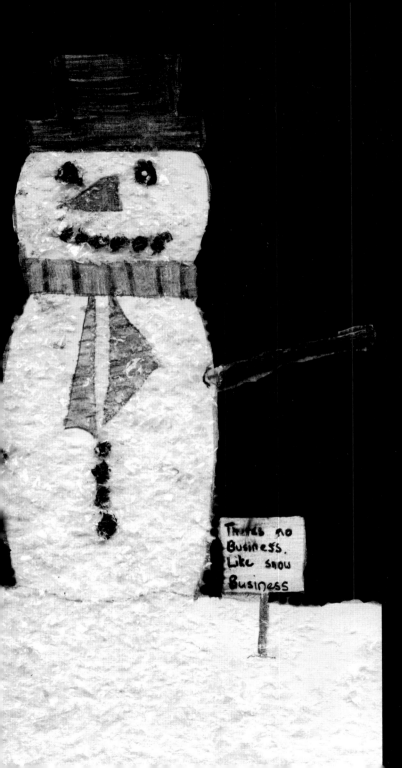

Darkness Is

Emma Keegan
St. Joseph's N.S Co. Westmeath

An attic in the night filled
with dust and spiders
Darkness is...
Going out-side in the night
with no moon or light to
guide you
Darkness is...
A whale coming towards
you in a wide-open sea
Darkness is...
Sitting at a table with no
one to talk to
Darkness is...
Being bullied and thrown
into the dark end of the
playground.

A Recipe For Becoming An Eagle

Darren Mc Loughlin
St. Joseph's N.S Co. Westmeath

Let your toenails grow long and then sharpen them to
look like talons.
Steal some feathers from a huge stuffed bird like an
Ostrich and glue them to your arm.
Go to the doctors and see if you have 20:20 vision.
Practise flying by jumping off a 60-story building,
And try not to kill yourself.
In the end if everything goes to plan,
Then you should be an eagle in no time at all.
But if everything goes horribly wrong,
Then too bad!

The River

Katie Daly
Cootehall N.S. Co. Roscommon

The river is the place we go
to watch the gentle waters flow

On this day so sunny and fine
Dad and I cast the fishing line

When the river is full of fish
it's my dads and mines greatest wish

Looking at the busy bees
buzzing round the evergreen trees

Down by the river in Cootehall
we would always welcome all.

Eagle by Ciara Keenan

Mo Mhúinteoir

Roibéaird O'Brien
Gaelscoil Bheanntraī, Bantry, Co. Cork

Ceapann mo mhúinteoir go bhfuil sí deas agus glick!!!!
Ach tugann sí alán abair bhaile duinn. Ach muinne bíonn
sé dínta seachtó fán cēad. Tēan a gruaige líeagh
Caitheann sí €14.00 shunē a chuir ar ais go dubh
Ach bíonn sí dens go léor
Mo mhúinteoir.

Dog by Eva Finn

My Dog

Caolán Carty
Cootehall N.S. Co. Roscommon

I have a dog,
He is brown and white,
His name is Bran,
He is my delight.

Each day at three,
Bran waits for me,
Beside our gate,
He knows if the bus is late.

He wags his tail,
And jumps with joy,
As I alight from the school bus,
Settle down boy!

Through the fields we run,
We have such fun.
We often play ball,
Bran jumps so tall!

Home we race,
Bran can keep the pace.
He sleeps all night long
Dawn arrives
Hurray! Away we go again for another day.

The Lonely Lion

Aaron Perrin
Cootehall N.S. Co. Roscommon

I'm a lonely lion in a pen.
People throwing litter at
me instead of in the bin
I hate being stuck in this zoo.
And I hate people looking at
me when I need to go to the
loo.

My Cat

Sinead Ní Cheibheannaigh
Gaelscoil Bheanntraí,
Bantry, Co. Cork

My cat hates baths.
I put her in some water
and she thought I was
going to slaughter her.
When I saw her the next
day she was very grumpy
I looked at her fur.
It was all bumpy and
I don't know why?
I let out a sigh.
Oh lovely kitty why can't
you stay pretty?

Monkey in the Jungle by Odhrán Johnson

Hurling And Football

Seán Ó Laoghaire
Gaelscoil Bheanntraí, Bantry, Co. Cork

My favourite hurling player is Joe Deane
He is so fast he can't be seen
Give him a free and it's over the bar
He can hit them from very far
My favourite football players are Graham Canty and
Noel O'Leary.
They are both deadly from a free
If they bury the ball the crowd go crazy
I guess by now you know I'm a Cork fan
So come on let's bring home Liam and Sam.

Smoking

Eibhlís Cadby
Gaelscoil Bheanntraí, Bantry, Co. Cork

I will never Smoke
Smoking is a Joke
People think it's cool
but really they are fools
It really harms your health
Especially your wealth
So my advice to you
Don't smoke your life down the loo.

House in the Forest by Nicole Griffin Healy

Two Dogs

Cáit Ní Bhriain
Gaelscoil Bheanntraí, Bantry, Co. Cork

I Once had a dog called Benjy
The Best dog and friend in the world
He had long smooth black and white fur
But his fuzzy ears were curled.

But then one day he got very sick
he had Alzheimer's and cancer too.
The next day when he died my first words
were 'I'll miss you.'

But now we have a new dog.
Susie is her name
You probably think I love her more but I love
Them both the same.

Stop Sammy, Drop it

Ciara Thornton
St. Columba's G.N.S Douglas

'Stop Sammy, Drop it'
Oh sorry about that,
I simply can't see why
I didn't get a cat.

'No Sammy, Bold.
That belongs to Dad
Oh Sammy for a dog
You really are bad'

'Give me my shoe!
It is not your toy
Drop it night now
You are such a bold boy!
I don't know what to do
I am at my wits' end
Sammy Oh Sammy
You drive me round the bend.'

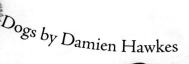

Dogs by Damien Hawkes

Dumb Glasses

Eoin Ó Donnchú
Gaelscoil Bheanntraí, Bantry, Co. Cork

I hate my glasses. They keep fogging up.
They are bent and ugly and so last century.
I wish they would break, I shiver ever time I have to put
them on.
They have to be taken off at lunchtime for fear they
would break. The serial number is 131313131366613666613.

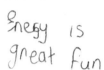

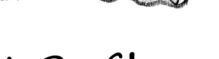

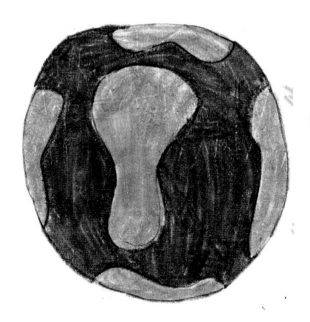

Save Our Planet! by Laura Doherty

One Minute Per Shower

Olivia Kiriposki
St. Columba's G.N.S Douglas

One minute per shower
You could take 60 in an hour
But one is all you need
So do it in high speed
And save the water.
I guess we ought to!!!

The Passion and Beauty

Claire O'Shea
St. Columba's G.N.S Douglas

The midnight breeze in the summer sky
The passion and beauty makes me fly
The wind in my hair
The light on my face
Makes me think of wonder and grace
I let myself dance
I twirl and I prance
My dress is flowing
The beauty is blowing
I walk to the beach
While the sky is still peach
When the sunset goes down
Goodbye to the passion
Goodbye to the beauty,
But won't you be here tomorrow
To fill my sorrow

I Love The Beach

Eve Radley
St. Columba's G.N.S Douglas

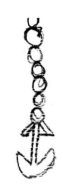

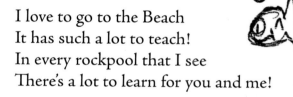

I love to go to the Beach
It has such a lot to teach!
In every rockpool that I see
There's a lot to learn for you and me!

Crabs and periwinkles,
Shrimp and fish
I found my first starfish and made a wish!

Along the beach I picked up a shell
I bet it has a story to tell!
There are lots of creatures to find
All so pretty and one of a kind!

As I sit upon the cliff and view the land
I see the ocean and miles and miles of sand
I love the beach...

The Sea by Ciara Ní Thuama

Standing In Destruction

Scott Duignan
St. Colmcille's N.S. Co. Longford

A Family in Burma wonder
Which direction to take
They cry and wonder
all around Burma
There isn't a village standing
So they keep looking
They can't find one
So they keep walking
They meet a family
The Family can't find their son.

Screaming by Keeva Dennehy

Ireland Is Anxious

Laura Healy
St. Colmcille's N.S Co. Longford

I can hear the cries in Burma
And see the tears in their eyes
I just want to help them.

Their standing on their own
I can hear their cries and moans
They have nowhere to go.

Ireland wants to help
I can see the disaster on tv
We will send out all we can

I need to do something
Ireland is anxious to help.

why is she screaming?

Mo Mhamaí

Síofra Ní Mháirtín
Gaelscoil Bheanntraí, Bantry, Co. Cork

Tú solas no shaol
Na fiado sa théal
Úll de mo shuil
An briseadh cúl

Grá ó mo chroí
Lán de sproi
Is tú mo mhamaí

Marvelous Mother

Áine Brady
St. Mary's N.S. Raharney Co. Westmeath

Marvelous mother, nice and kind
Outstanding, cheerful and wise
Tender and loving in every way
Helpful and happy every day
Enthusiastic in everything you do
Rare mam, I love you.

Dancing by Sarah Fogarty

My Favourite Sport

Roisín Clarke
St. Columba's G.N.S Douglas

My favourite sport is camogie
This sport is quite tough
So therefore I must be quite rough
If the ball is going high
I try to catch it from the sky
When I lash it on the floor
I hope to get a score!!!

Camogie by Maryanne Hegarty

Chocolate

Níamh O'Leary
St. Columba's G.N.S Douglas

Milk, caramel, dark & creamy
All together make me dreamy
Shaped, smooth, crunchy or sweet.
Either way it's delicious to eat.
I try to keep my mind on learning
But I can't help this constant yearning,
Just a square or two will do
Maybe you could try it too!

Pirate's Treasure

Adam Dalton
St. Brendan's N.S. Tralee, Co. Kerry

Plundering pirates we love to be
Islands for burying treasure far out to sea
Rampaging rascals is what we are
Attacking all ships near and far
Traders and merchants have to be aware
Escaping every trap and snare
Sword fighting with seamen every where.

Parrot in the Mirror by Maha Khurshid

The Navigator

Jack O'Connor
St. Brendan's N.S. Tralee, Co. Kerry

I love to look out on the sea,
Because it means so much to me,
I love to hear the wild waves roar,
And watch them racing to the shore.
And Brendan on his hill so high,
Commands the waves as they pass by,
I'm sure he thinks about the days
When he was sailing on those waves.
He casts an ever watchful eye,
On all who sail and pass him by.
My school is blessed with Brendan's name
A saint and sailor of great fame,
Encased in bronze he stands alone,
This weary sailor rests at home.

Pirate

Zoe O'Carroll
St. Brendan's N.S. Tralee, Co. Kerry

Pirate of the deep blue sea,
In his ship he is free,
Roving through the
treacherous tides,
Always his parrot by
his side,
Treasure is all that's on his mind,
Eye patch and 'Jolly Rogger'
are his signs.

Shark by Kate Hedderman

My Donkey

Shannon Higgins
Moyvore N.S. Co. Westmeath

A four legged lawn mower
Eating grass all day
But when the grass doesn't grow
I give him some hay.

He has big brown eyes,
Long brown ears,
Four big strong legs
But has never shed any tears.

The animal I am talking about
Is a favourite pet of mine
And when he needs to be brushed
I've always got the time.

The Neva Looks Back

Nicole O'Connor
Mount Temple N.S. Co. Westmeath

The Neva looks back to me
it talks to me
it says 'you fish in me every day
You eat my fish
and drink my water
When I run out of fish
where will you go?'
I said 'when you run out of fish
I will still come to you
for the beauty of your river.'

Fish by Leah O'Keeffe

The Grizzly Bear

Aoife Connolly
Scoil Ursula, Strandhill Rd. Sligo

One day I was being so good
So my friend and I went for
A walk in the wood

We weren't walking that fast.
O how I wish it would last,
But standing over there
Was a huge grizzly bear.
With his huge sharp teeth
And his big bear like feet
He gave a big growl
And I let out a howl.
That was the end of
Me and my dear friend.

Grizzly by Sophie O'Callaghan

Wolf

Alex Moorhead
Moyvore N.S. Co. Westmeath

The wolf is strong.
It drags me along.
The rugged path to life.

Bedtime

Aoife O'Neill
Scoil Ursula, Blackrock, Cork

Every night I go to bed,
I just lay down and rest my sleepy head.

I also hug my teddy bear,
But only to get over my fears.

There's a monster that is huge and scary,
That's why I hug my teddy named Bearie.

I run and I scream,
From the monster that is big and green.

Every night I go to bed,
I lay down and rest my sleepy head.

Wolf by Patrick Collins

My Little Brother

David Stone
St. Oliver Plunkett B.N.S. Co Westmeath

My little brother's crazy,
That's all I have to say,
And when he wakes up in the morning
We're in for another chaotic day.

He'd run around the garden,
He'd run around the town,
He'd run, punch, scream and yell,
We just can't calm him down

Once he shaved the dog,
A mohican on the top,
My dog wasn't laughing,
But my brother could not stop

As time goes by,
We are yet to find a cure
He might be normal again,
But with him, you can't be sure.

As you might have noticed,

He causes me to stress,
For he cannot do a thing,
Other than make a mess.

He never stops talking,
It drives my family mad,
Sometimes it drives me crazy,
Sometimes it makes me sad.

It's my brother's way of fun,
He thinks it's just a joke,
But the heart of the problem is...
Too many cans of coke!!!

Boy by Sophie Tuffy

The Calf

Michael Lavin
Grange N.S. Boyle Co. Roscommon

The calf in the shed
that I thought was dead
Is alive as could be
He is here with me
When I go to the shed
He is always waiting there
Open mouth to be fed
Begging for care
I give him the bottle
And he is out of despair.

I am 5

I Have To Go Now

Julien Torrades
High Park N.S Co. Sligo

Life was such a mystery
a mystery everyday
although there were some bad times
the best were the hurrays
I remember how to speak
Or playing hiding go seek
I remember playing with my friends
But I just hoped
Those times to never end
I learned lots of playing in my tots
I learned how to share
Or when I started to care
Being a child was really really wild
Running through the bushes
Was as cool as the rushes
But that was all in the past
I thought they were a blast
Now I'm under a grave
I hope my grandchildren will behave.

I am 6

Girls by Zuzana Kotz and Margaret Szczurowska

68

Bubbles

Michael Broder
St. Mary´s N.S. Raharney Co. Westmeath

Bubbles, bubbles, everywhere,
And not a bubble to burst
So if I want to burst a bubble,
I will have to blow some first.

Bubbles

Robert Coyne
St. Mary´s N.S. Raharney Co. Westmeath

I blow bubbles in the sun,
It´s such a lot of fun.

Big and round,
Till they burst,
On the ground

Then—splat,
wet,
flat.

Singing Birds by Gabrielle Viana de Sousa

Fighting the Monster by Gabriel Moreira Dos Santos

The Bully

Shane Kelly
High Park N.S Co. Sligo

I know a kid called Jim who's big and tall
He loves to see other kids fall
He will pull a girls hair and make her cry
Or push her on the ground and there she'll lie.

This boy is mean and takes kids money
Because he is big and thinks he is funny
He thinks he is strong but he is not
Because no friends he has got.

Why does he act in this way?
I'm sure he will learn his lesson one day
When another kid comes along who's bigger than him
'What did I do?' will be asked by Jim.

I Often Land in Trouble

Ellen Kiernan Molloy
St. Mary's N.S. Granard Co. Longford

I often Land in Trouble
It's not the best way
to start the day.
If I'm told to do something
I often walk away.

When The Wig Is On My Head

Aisling Cunningham
St. Marys N.S. Granard Co. Longford

When the wig is on my head
It feels so heavy
It is hard to dance
When the wig is on my head

I have to prepare everything
like fake tan and even make up.

The fake tan has to go on the night before
If I don't it will show no colour.

I love being an Irish dancer
but if I don't follow
the rules of wearing tan and make up
I'll be disqualified.

Horse in the Sun by Victoria Kingston

Summer

Katlyn Hurley
Scoil Ursula, Blackrock, Cork

Sun burning
Under the shade of trees
Most of my holidays at the beach
Maybe some sun block would be handy
Everyday gets hotter and hotter
Running freely through the green blades of grass.

A Word For The World

Laura Sweeney
Aughavas, Carrigallan N.S. Co. Leitrim

What's gone wrong
with the world
There's bombs in Iraq
and people on crack
Oh what's gone wrong with the world
People losing importance
when they don't get
affection and suffer rejection.
Oh what's gone wrong
with the world.
Then there's people
Drunk Dancing to crazy Funk
Oh what's gone wrong with the world.

The Face of the Flower

Declan Farley
St. Colmcille's N.S. Co. Longford

The face of the flower
makes us all glow
It makes us feel happy.

The face of the flower
shines so bright all year
It is so bright and yellow
like a god dressed in yellow.

Flower by Faiza Raja

On Our Farm

Rebecca Tierney
Aughavas N.S., Carrigallan, Co. Leitrim

Our farm
Has baby chicks
Hens clucking
Cows mooing for silage
Calves in and out

through the barriers,
Playing with the other calves
they want to be free
running in the fields
As free as a bee buzzing around.
The tractor on a Saturday
rolling, topping, spraying the fields
Spreading fertilizer or slurry
The hens running around,
looking for insects
The roosters crowing
The hens in the sand,
putting sand in their feathers

The four heifers
out in the fields
kicking their hind-legs
waiting for nuts or maybe
fresh water,
The bulls just over the road
running, jumping
These animals will thrive
this is what they want,
The cat on the hay,
snoozing away,
This is my life
I never want to change it
This is my word for the world.

Tractors by Daniel Curley

I Look Behind Me

Amy Conboy
Aughavas N.S., Carrigallan, Co. Leitrim

I look behind me
Into the crowd
All the movement, all the sound
But what do they all think?
What do they all feel?
They need to crack a smile
And feel what is real!
All the sizes, all the shapes
But why are they not standing up straight?
If they don't feel happy,
If they don't feel great
Then, what future,
Will await?

Something Special

Jessica Bohan
Aughavas N.S. Carrigallan, N.S. Co. Leitrim

There's something special in my house
I'm sure it's a mouse
because in the hall
there is a hole in the wall
its suspiciously small
I cover the hole up with my clothes
So my Mam can't smell it with her nose
and if she does she'll throttle him yet
But, 'Mam,' I say, 'I want to keep him as my pet!'

Witch by Eilish Murray

My Mother's Frying Pan

James Byrne
Killashee, N.S. Co Longford

My mother's Frying pan.
It is black and grey.
When I hear the sausage
sizzle I know
It's that time of day.
It comes once a week
on a Saturday Morning
Toast and sausages
with bacon and beans.

I Fix A Ladder

Darragh Scott
St. John´s N.S. Battery rd, Longford

I fix a ladder
With nails and hammer
With my hard work.
I don't care
If I get cuts, bumps and bruises
All that matters
Is getting the job done.

Tree by Mary Walsh

75

I Pull Myself Together

Ruairí Nerney
Killashee, N.S. Co Longford

I pull myself together.
When I'm told
to achieve something better
for when I'm older

It's great to be a good,
So fresh so good mannered,
So others will like me intensely.

My Colours Run

Kelley Bennett
St. John's N.S., Battery rd., Longford

My colours run together,
Inside of me
I can feel the anger of red.
The peacefulness of white
The emptiness of black
And girly feeling of pink.

Leopard and Hunter by Carrie Ahern

Never Seen Rain

Evie Moloney
St. John's N.S., Battery rd., Longford

The little boy watched in wonder
As clouds filled the sky
The little boy with nothing
Watched the clouds fill the sky
As those clouds went from
Blue...to grey.

The little boy with nothing
Was filled with great happiness
As many people gathered together
To watch the clouds fill the sky.

As the little boy looked up
He saw his mother and father
Stare down from above
When the clouds went from
Blue...to grey.

The little boy with nothing,
Was filled with great joy,
As the rain fell from the sky.

I Will Never Understand

Jack Cullen
St. Patricks B.N.S Ballinamore
Co. Leitrim

I will never understand
why it all happened
why they were shot
Why they died
I will never understand.

Inside My Playhouse

Lisa Nolan
Cloontagh N.S. Longford

Inside my playhouse
I'm away from the world
I like to play shop
I don't like to be disturbed.
When my brother comes in
he pretends to be a cop
I feed him plastic food and
he spits them on the floor.

Playing on the Street by Sophie Gray

Lying On The Trampoline

Alannah Dolan
Cloontagh N.S. Longford

I'm lying on the trampoline
Watching the clouds
It is so peaceful
I can't hear the cows.

I'm lying on the trampoline.
Not hearing a sound.
My mother is calling
But I am too interested in what I found.

I Like Inbetween

Shannon Boyle
Scoil Mhuire N.S. Bornacoola, Co. Leitrim

I like my tea inbetween.
Not too milky not too sweet
always from a different cup.

I like my days inbetween
Not so sunny and not so dull.
And everyday there's something different.

I like myself inbetween
I'm not too mean and not too sweet
And everyday I'm glad I'm me.

I've Never Had A Cappuccino

Orla MacSweeney
Scoil Mhuire N.S. Bornacoola, Co. Leitrim

I've never had a cappuccino
up on the board it looks
smooth and delicious,
I see it in the café
pouring out into a mug
looking thick and yummy!
I wonder why?
It looks so heavenly
It makes me hungry
Next time I want a cappuccino.

Freaky Sun by Ania Gwidrd

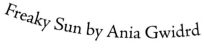

79

Sitting On Today

Emilie Dugdale
Hunt N.S Mohill

I drew myself
sitting on today
holding a future.
dreaming of a world.
that's too perfect to be true.

Sitting on today
I'll just begin now
making this moment
as happy as can be.
I look out on the first
May day.

Beware Of The Man

Shauna McCrann
Fatima N.S. Cloone, Co. Leitrim

'Beware of the man'
Mam says
Whose eyebrows meet

'Beware of the man'
Mam says
Whose eyebrows meet
For in his heart
Lies deceit.

Beware of the girl
whose mam is very careful
She's always by her side.

Friends by Angel Rowley

80

His Tail Up In The Air

Megan O'Donnell
Aughnasheelin N.S. Ballinamore, Co. Leitrim

With his tail up in the air,
Lying there without a care,
He doesn't have to hunt for food,
His tail is in the air.

He's lying on my bed,
Chasing cats around his head,
He is lying on my bed.

He wants to go to sleep,
Close his eyes without a peep,
Snuggling in my purple sheets,
He wants to go to sleep.

I don't mind him lying there,
With his tail up in the air,
He doesn't have to hunt for food,
His tail is in the air.

Cat by Sarah McGlone

Kynät

Jaro Koho
Aarnivalkean koulu, Espoo, Finland

Kynät ovat tylsiä
Se alkaa kyrsiä
Sitten niitä alkaa jyrsiä

Kyniä pitää teroittaa
Muuten alkaa potuttaa
Ja se suututtaa

Kynät ovat myös hyödyllisiä
Niillä voi kirjoittaa
Tarinoita yöllisiä

Let Me Out

Calvin Jones
St. John's N.S. Edgeworthstown, Co. Longford

'Let me out!' the words scream
Stupid sisters, stupid prince
If I didn't love the prince
I wouldn't be in this mess
The kind fairy heard her cry
While the wind went floating by.

Fairies by Fiona Power

The Truth Is I'm Superstitious

Stephen Courtney
St. Dominics N.S. Kenagh Co. Longford

The Truth is I'm superstitious
I never stand on cracks.

The Truth is I'm superstitious
I also hate black cats.

The truth is I'm superstitious
I hate Friday the 13th.

I hate being superstitious
It makes me want to scream.

Always being afraid of something
that probably isn't real.

On A Lonely Day

Hazel Fleming
Mount Temple N.S. Co. Westmeath

On a lonely day
sitting on the couch,
watching television
I'm getting bored of that

Looking out the window
Rain is spilling down,
Nothing else to do
except keep my feet off the ground!

On A Foolish Day

Adrian Claffey
Mount Temple N.S. Co. Westmeath

On a foolish day
I come in at the end
And eat my tea
and watch something on RTE

Girls by Jess Maclachlan

Working For A Vote

Darren Keegan
Fatima N.S. Cloone, Co. Leitrim

Don't vote for him.
Don't vote for any of them.
Vote for me.
I'm all around Leitrim
On gates, fences, poles and lampposts
Waiting for your vote.

When The Computer Is OFF

David Hudson
St. John's N.S. Edgeworthstown, Co. Longford

When the Computer is OFF
I feel like I am OFF
I have no fun
nothing to do
Yet homework is always there.

Minnie Mouse by Shannen Kearney

Into The Mouth of the River

Eleanor Lisle
Fermoyle N.S. Co. Longford

Into the mouth of the river
The ship went sailing away
Going up and down up and down.
Sailing out far, far away.

The wind is fierce
The waves are hard.
The ship jumps every time we hit a wave.
I feel like I am in a grave,
Like I'm in the air.
with butterflies in my stomach.

Finaly Dublin is on the horizon
With me shining in front.
Jumping for Joy with a smile on my face.

Dublin's Coming Into Sight

Niall Nolan
Fermoyle N.S. Co. Longford

Dublin's coming into sight
As we come down the North Sea
We can see seagulls flying
Over Dublin bay.

The seagull screech
The waves crash
Into the side of the boat
The wind blows so hard.

She gallops over the waves
As she done 1000 years ago
The boat feels at home
I know, because I can feel it too

Yachts by Pedro Luis Medina

Yellow Hailstones

Áine Lynch
St. Columba's N.S. Dring,
Co. Longford

Yellow hailstones falling from
the sky
All the grass cut and rolled
to make the farmer high.

The farmer sees yellow
hailstones
falling from the sky
He wants to call everyone
But there's no one around.

Saving Our Planet And Getting A Green Flag

Laura Doherty
St. Mary's N.S. Raharney Co. Westmeath

Have a quick shower
Save on power
Turn off the lights
Open the blinds
Cut down on packaging
Use less wrapping.

Recycling, Recycling
Is so much fun...
We all worked hard
And our school won!

In the Shower by Amy Turpin

My Toy Dinosaur

Ciaran Tumulty
Ard Keenan N.S. Drum Co. Westmeath

My toy dinosaur
is ten centimetres tall
It's a T.Rex
It scares my sister.
It can roar and move
and my brother isn't afraid
He just knocks it over
and laughs at it
My toy dinosaur
attacks my sister
she runs to her room
then I turn it off.

The Doll On The Page

Jennifer Duignan
Ard Keenan N.S. Drum Co. Westmeath

She's all along the page
and she's coming alive
She looks around
but there's no one she can talk to
So she's trying to come
out of the page and start a new life
she finds a door.

Circus Ponies by Corinne Gondouini

Making The Tree

Danielle Kelly
Sacred Heart N.S. Granard Co. Longford

I remember making the tree
Teacher said it was good
If I had more time
I would have put more effort in
Teacher put it on the wall
I was happy but kept thinking
to myself it's bad
Not as good as the other trees.

Trees

Rachel Gallagher
Scoil Bhride, Eglantine, Douglas Cork

Branches spread big and wide.
The perfect place for me to hide.
Climb up high to the top,
As you go the ground will drop.
'I have reached the top, phew,
but I'm glad I did it, look at the view!!
I can see everywhere.'
Feel the wind ripple through my hair.
Branches spread big and wide.
Tress are the perfect place to hide.

The Tree and The Mountain by Leanne Finn

The Tree

THe Mountain

Lying On The Ground

Cathal Shields
Ard Keenan N.S. Drum Co. Westmeath

Lying on the ground
Playing with my cars
Pushing them not too far
Looking inside
At every little detail
That hides.

Eating On The Couch

Ruaidhrí McManus
Ard Keenan N.S. Drum Co. Westmeath

I like eating on the couch
Sometimes I leave crumbs on the floor.
And my Mam gets thick with me
Sometimes I just lie there
and relax and rest and think of lovely places,
where everything is so silent and beautiful.

The Flower by Rebecca Doody

I Am A Vampire

Aisling Brady
Scoil Mhuire Gan Smal, Lanesboro, Co. Longford

I'm a Vampire
tall and strong
my lips are red
and my hair is long.

I suck your blood
Dark and red
if you don't watch
out I'll cut off your head.

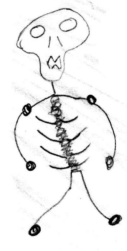

I love my life
without the sun
to live in the dark
can be so much fun.

Skeletons by Sarah Keohane

The Bully

Killian Doyle
St. Mary's N.S. Raharney Co. Westmeath

I went to school feeling good
until I met the bully.
The bully was big, tall and strong,
And had a group of lads with him.
Who thought they had it all
Bullying little children and
pranking everyone.
Until one day I told the teacher,
Who did not care so the bully lived on!

Being In Trouble

Donal Mullen
St. Mary's N.S. Raharney Co. Westmeath

When I do something bad
I get in trouble.
My Mum shouts and stamps her
feet at me,
Then she wags her finger.
My Dad goes half crazy
But I don't talk at all
I bite my tongue
And wait till it all settles down.

The Louvre by Denise O'Kelly

Children Of All Colours

Shane Gorman
St. Mary's N.S. Raharney Co. Westmeath

It is the year 2008,
As I go out and open my gate,
I look around and see before me
Children of every colour united as one
In this our small country.

We mix in our school yard
And play the same games
There's no real difference
Except for our unusual names!

Confusion

Claire Coyne
St. Mary's N.S. Raharney Co. Westmeath

If my confusion is your confusion
Then how confused you must be
For my confusion confuses me
To the point where I can't see!

And if your confusion
Confuses me
As mine confuses you
Then the two of us
Must be confused
As to who is confusing who!

Camel by Sophie Tuffy

Dear Cliona And Andrea

Sara Turnbull
Scoil Bhride, Eglantine, Douglas Cork

The weather's terrible at this summer camp
The food is awful
The teachers are gloomy
Sleeping in a cold tent
Clothes never dry
Boots too big
Having to walk outside to the bathroom at night
No hair-brush in sight
Teeth gone yellow
No friends at all not even a marsh mallow
No sitting around the camp fire at night just going to bed on a
gloomy day
I have to say I will be lucky if I can survive the next day
Hope to see you in school and may be I will be ok.
From your friend Sara
P.s. Do you want to come with me next year?

Wind

Dean Core
St. Mary´s N.S. Raharney
Co. Westmeath

Can't see it,
But you can hear it!
Can't beat it,
But you can feel it!
Soft and gentle,
Or strong and wild,
Gale or hurricane,
A breeze is mild.
Wind is mild.
Wind is freedom–
Freedom to fly my kite.

Balloon Party! by Nikita Narang

93

Can Anybody Hear Me?

Kate Mac Sweeney
Scoil Bhride, Eglantine, Douglas Cork

It was a dark and dreary night
The sirens were hurting my ears
We moved house to get away from war
But now it was closing in on my fears
The sky was turning red to me
As the planes flew overhead
There were so many people around me
But all of them were dead
Rubble and ash was all
That was left of our little town
And I searched for my family everywhere
In my bloodstained nightgown
All the cars were lit alight
The smell of petrol filled the air
My arm was terribly sore
But I really didn't care
I knew that I had to help
I called 'Can anybody hear me'
But no one gave a yelp
I went into my burning house
And to my discover
I found my parents under planks of wood
But I knew they wouldn't recover
I ran outside again

As I nearly gave up hope
I felt I wouldn't be able to deal with the result
I just simply couldn't cope
So as I finish up this poem
I have one last thing to say
I still have nightmares about it
That horrible night and day.

Soldiers At The Front

Elaine Kingston
Scoil Bhride, Eglantine, Douglas Cork

Lining up
In straight rows
Why they're fighting
No one knows.

Roll of honour
They fall like flies
Family reassuring them
But it's all lies

When war is over
And fighting done
We'll start a new one
Like the first one
Had never begun.

The Beauty Of The World

Rachel Hinds
Scoil Bhride, Eglantine, Douglas Cork

The beauty of the land and sea,
Is in the end a mystery.
On something that we now share,
In a thousand years may not be there.
But I do love the sun when rising,
Or a wasp in a flower–How surprising!
The colours of the coral reef,
The rise to the air, the gasp of relief
The scent of a fir tree, the buzz of a bee,
The treasure down beneath the sea.
The sway of grass in the cool summer breeze,
Or the twitter of creatures within the trees.
But, the most beautiful thing on the earth,
All a lifetime is it worth.
The best thing in the world we know,
Are the colours of a rainbow.

Ringed Plover by John O'Callaghan

Galmoy

Mary Corcoran
St. Michaels N.S. Galmoy, Co. Kilkenny

Galmoy is my favourite place,
It is the place to be.
We have a church we have a hall.
It's where I want to be
Some people think its kind of small
But I think it's big,
Because I'm with my friends
It's there I want to be.

Our Principal

Amy Coles
Scoil na nAingeal Naofa, Co. Roscommon

Our principal is really cool
He's the master of our school.
Good or bad he's always there
Making he's presence felt
Everywhere.
Up and down the corridor he paces
Just to keep us in our places
Always singing sometimes dancing
Our principal is always prancing
Always gentle never snappy that's
Why
Our school is really happy.
We love our school!!!

Wakacje

Małgosia Siepiera
Zespól Szkół, Gdansk, Poland

Pojechałam na wakacje
po nowe wrażenia
i nowe atrakcje,
w oceanu pływać falach
chciałam
tańczyć też na balach
chciałam
jeździć ma rowerze
trochę nudzić się w operze
pławić się w promieniach słońca
i przeczytać też do końca

szkolną lekturę

odłożyłam ją
na dni deszczowe i ponure
ale dni takich nie było
więc na ,,chceniu´´
się skończyło

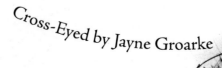

Cross-Eyed by Jayne Groarke

Smiling Heart by Ruth Moriarty

Snowman by Kerrie Anne Murtagh

WOW by Zara Weir

Armadillo by Paddy Creegan

98

Duckling by Hollie Martin

Mr Spud by Sara Turnbull

99

Man in a Fez by Zara Conway

Cheetah by Clíodhna Buckley

House by Eleanor O'Connell

Birthday Party by Michelle Mc Guinn

102

Sunflowers by Laura Haurican

Palm Trees by Emma Daly

Sunflower by Anna Harte

Seahorse by Shauna Conlon

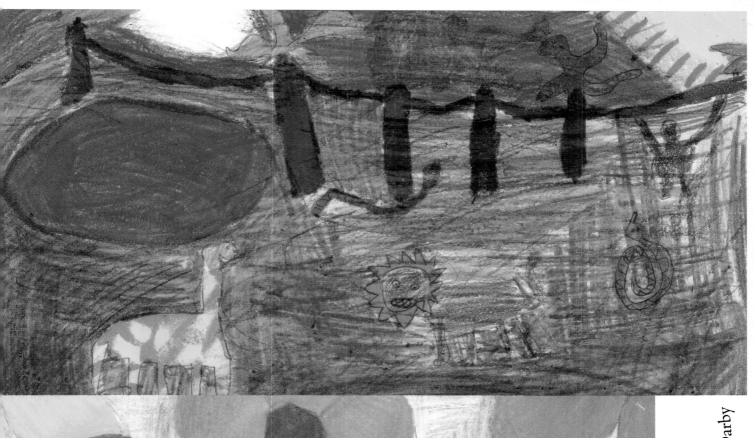

Lion and Giraffe by Leanne Darby

Spring by Amy Evans

Dolphins by Clionagh Murphy

Garden by Nina Doroganá

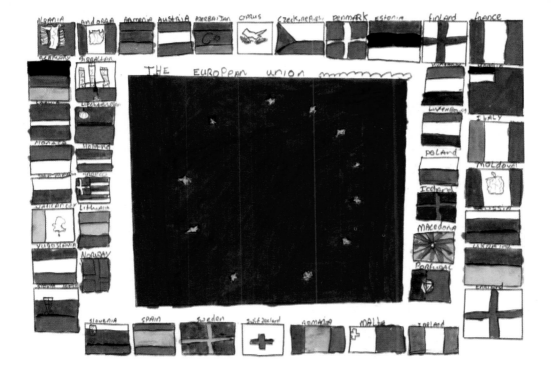

EU Flags by Evan Galvin

Surfing by Carla Benson

Daffodil by Sinéad Simpson

Horse Grazing by Aoife Moore

Rainbow by Jamie Duignan   Balloons by Lauren Crawford   Girl by Siobhan Tighe

Black Cat by Hannah-Mae Grainger

Playground by Aioghna O'Leary

Dots and Spots by Laura Patton

Car by Conor Loftus

Puss by Stephanie Marrion

Owl by Jack Tierney

My Mum And My Housework

Sinéad Meehan
Scoil na nAingeal Naofa, Co. Roscommon

My mum does housework day after day,
While we are out playing our games.
She cooks the dinner, cleans the house
And makes sure we get out.
My mum is like a cleaning machine,
Polishing windows and the T.V.
She never gets time for herself
Only cleaning everything else.
I don't know why she cleans so much
She always makes a fuss.
My mum is like a cleaning machine,
I hate when it's time for Spring cleaning.

Rhyme

Siobhán Jordan
Brierfield NS, Co. Galway

I want to write
A poem
That isn't going to
Rhyme.
That's why I've been
Sitting here.
Four hours at a time

Oh no!
My poem rhymed.
I'm determined not to make my poem
Rhyme.
So it won't

My Mum and Me by Jasmine Forde

Diamante Poem

Aoife Lyons
Ovens N.S, Co. Cork

Girls
Nice polite
Skipping, running, playing
Innocent, mannerly, rude, loud
Shouting, hiking, punching
Bold, troublesome
Boys.

Love

Aoife O'Sullivan
Ovens N.S, Co. Cork

I make people go head over heels
I make people write on trees!!!
Lonely goes away when I come along
and everyone listens when I sing a song!!

Punk Rocker by Adrienne Rawle

I Play The Drum

Eoin Sorohan
Fermoyle N.S. Co. Longford

I play the Drum
In the school band.
I keep the beat
when it's on its stand.

I play the drum
through the night
Booming in the moonlight
until it's bright.

Running All The Way

Ciaran Byrne
Rossan, N.S. Carrigallen, Co. Leitrim

She hops on a train
And can't stop thinking
About Grandfather,
As the steam escapes
Out of the train
Like a wild elephant
Running from the zoo.

She hops on a train
And somersaults through a song
Through all the lyrics
Over all the notes,
Loving Grandfather.

Snagglepuss by Nicole Griffin Healy

Outdoors

Emma Flanagan
Scoil na nAingeal Naofa, Co. Roscommon

As I climb up the tree
What a beautiful site I see
I see a swan in the lake
In the rushes is a tall drake.

As I come down the tree
The leaves blow in the breeze
My mum said to me
Come in now or you will freeze.

Garden by Ava Sisk

Autumn

Rachel Byrne
Scoil na nAingeal Naofa, Co. Roscommon

Today as I sit here, using my
Doorstep as a chair, the birds sit
Quietly upon my fence as if saying
A prayer.

The clouds are huge and white but
None we'll be seeing here tonight.
My cat goes by chasing a fly,
But she will never get him no matter
How she tries.

The leaves are falling off the trees.
The flowers are going to bed.
This is a sign that winter nights
Are ahead.

My Hospital Diary

Shannon Ashmore
Scoil na nAingeal Naofa, Co. Roscommon

When I was born I was so weak that
They baptised me in hospital, the Coombe,
Then a heart operation after three weeks,

Thankfully then I began to grow Strong…
after a time period that seemed very long
until I was seven and had to go hospital again
but lucky for me the Doctors there
were as good as can be.

Now I'm older and I am doing well
my ticker is ticking.

After my big operation my daddy
Brought me home
I felt I was safer there
But I still had the fear of returning again
with not a break of even a year.

Dog by Shannon Kerins

Abandoned And Neglected Dog

Keela Grâda,
Scoil Mhuire Wellington Rd, Cork

Animal cruelty
Why are they the ones
who have to suffer.
Why are they the ones who get
abandoned and neglected.

Why are they the ones who
get treated like rubbish.
Why are we the ones that
live happily ever after.

Horses, dogs whatever.
Help to stop these
poor creatures suffer,
They've had enough.

Smile

Tonichia Suffin
Scoil na nAingeal Naofa, Co. Roscommon

A smile is broad and tall,
It tells everyone you're happy.

A smile is warm and caring,
To cheer someone up when they're sad.

A smile is for everyone,
So try it out and you will see,
What fun it can be

Sunny Scene by Cathal O'Dowd

I Bite My Nails

Tanya Mc Guinn
Scoil na nAingeal Naofa, Co. Roscommon

I bite my nails at tea time
I bite my nails at lunch
I bite my nails at dinner
I must never have enough.

I bite my nails when I'm playing
I bite my nails when I'm working
I bite my nails when I'm sleeping
And even when I'm dreaming.

I bite my nails watching TV.
I bite them every evening.
I bite my nails in the shower and
Guess what? I'm biting them now!

My Sister

Claudia McLoughlin
Scoil na nAingeal Naofa, Co. Roscommon

I have a little sister,
She's only nine years old
And whenever she's asked to do something
She never does what she's told.

I have a little sister,
And sometimes she's a pain
Whenever I ask her for something
She always has to complain.

I have a little sister
And she can be so sweet
Whenever she gives me a hug
I get her a little treat.

I have a little sister
And she can be so crazy
But another thing's for sure
She can also be very lazy.

My Little Brother

Saoirse Noone
Scoil na nAingeal Naofa, Co. Roscommon

Little hands and little feet,
Big blue eyes and smile so sweet
Softest hair that shines like gold
My little brother is one year old.

Sticky handprints on the door
Lots of toys all over the floor
Ma-ma da-da goo-goo gaa-gaa
My little brother I'm glad of that.

Tired eyes lie down to sleep
Till the morning not a peep
Little angel sweet sweet dreams
My little brother
Forever will be.

Hands

Eve Burke
Scoil na nAingeal Naofa, Co. Roscommon

Hands are things we use everyday,
We use them to write, to feel, to play,
They help us to pick up all sorts of things,
And put plasters on swollen bee stings.

Hands can help us to open up books,
To hit people when they give us nasty looks,
They help us to open up lollipops,
And push back hair that's beginning to flop.

Hands are things we use everyday,
We use them to write, to feel, to play.

Hedgehog by Adam Lockhart

Listen To Your Mother

Caoimhe Morris
Scoil na nAingeal Naofa, Co. Roscommon

Listen to your mother
Because she's always right
Listen to your mother
And she'll set you right

She'll tell you lots of things
That you need to know
Like how to boil an egg
And make some buttery toast

She'll tell you lots of stories
Of when she was young
And how things have changed
Now the years have rolled on

Listen to your mother
And you grandmother too
They have lots of life experiences
To share with you

The Money Tree

Linda Mannion
Brierfield NS, Co. Galway

I sowed money in the garden
And went to bed that night
When I woke up in the morning
I got such a fright

I opened the curtains
And in front of me
Waving its branches
Was a money tree

There were fivers and tenners
And twenty pounds notes
I planed to buy houses,
Fast cars and boats

All of a sudden
There blew up a gale
Thunder and lightning
And big stones of hail

Out of the tree
The money took flight
Over the hills
And soon out of sight

I gazed at the tree
Where the money had been
And thought to myself
Was it all just a dream?

Básnička o básničce

Viktor Matějka
Gymnázium Jiřího Ortena, Kutná Hora

Když jsem včera pařil,
nepřátele mařil,
na básničku zapomněl.
Ráno s hrůzou zjišťuji,
že v sešitě nic nestojí,
ale teď musím do školy.
Po cestě básním,
verše vymýšlím,
dál už to nevím,
budoucnost nevěstím.

The Tree by Marco Gavrila

121

Water

Scott Weir
Brierfield NS, Co. Galway

Life-giver
Life-taker
Home-giver
Home-breaker
Boat-floater
Boat-sinker
Finger-wrinkler
Toe-tingler
Thirst-quencher
Hose-sprinkler
Engine-cooler
Body-washer

A Day In The Bog

Eoin Loftus
Brierfield NS, Co. Galway

My father called us early,
He said 'Get up ye sleepy heads
Were off to the bog in Abbert,
Get out of them Bunk beds'.

Dad drove us there in the pick-up
But I drove down the bog road.
It's my favourite spot in the whole
Wide world it's where you might see
a toad.

We turned the turf, though it was soggy,
We knew, that it would dry
All around was bog cotton and heather,
Later we went home for a fry.

Best Friends by Kelly Ruxton

My Hot Water Bottle

Eamon Mannion
Brierfield NS, Co. Galway

A rubber sensation
Some call it a jar
It keeps the bed warm
Wherever you are

Fill with hot water
And turn the lid tight
There's nothing more to it
You're warm for the night

My Gran uses one
To warm her two feet
It's covered in fur
To keep in the heat

My sister had one
It was fluffy and red
But one night it burst
And wet the whole bed

So it's out with the old
And in with the new
These new plug-in blankets
Will just have to do

Monsters

Anthony Ryan
Scoil Mhuire Lourdes, Carrigaline, Cork

Some monsters are big some monsters are small my monster is the right size and a trouble maker too. He runs around breaking windows. He takes food from shops. He runs across the Sahara dessert. He swims to Antarctica and comes back with a mouth full of fish. He hates doing home work and he hates doing chores and he hates fruit and vegetables. He loves sport and candy and he loves playing videos games and loves playing with his cousins. He went to Mexico where his cousins live. They played lots of games and when he came home his two cousins came back with him. He asked his Mom if they could stay and she said yes. Then nearly everyone moved out.

Monster by Anthony Ryan

What Makes A Good Friend!

Megan Carr
Brierfield NS, Co. Galway

A good friend to me should be trustworthy
And kind
And I don't think that would be very
Hard to find.

A great mate to me should be
Honest and fun.
Yes with a heart so friendly
Like the warm summer sun!

Bunt

Matti Behnke
Grundschule an der Bake, Mönkeberg

Die Blumen
Sie blühen auf
Bunte Farben leuchten hell
Schön!

Girl by Eilish Murray

The Lie

Liam Henry
Scoil Ursula, Strandhill Rd. Sligo

It wasn't me I had to say,
Everybody was staring at me that day.
Could I lie once again.
Or could I say it was him.

That very next day I was in the same position.
But I decided not to lie,
I got in trouble,
And just thought.
Why didn't I lie

Lies by Liam Henry

Ruusu

Lotta Kaijärvi
Aarnivalkean koulu, Espoo, Finland.

Punainen
Ruusu
Suloinen ja kaunis
Kasvaa rakkauden puutarhassa
Yksin

Dancing Fairies

Kelly Lynch
Scoil Ursula, Blackrock, Cork

When the rain hits the floor
It's like fairies dancing
There for a split second
But still so beautiful.

Bingo

Shannon White
Scoil Ursula, Blackrock, Cork

I better make this short and sweet,
Not much time to waste,
Numbers being called out fast
I'm down to one number at last
Come on number 8
I'm going to be late for my date
Oh yes yes here it comes
Bingo

Motorbikes by Damien Hawkes

Dad

Denise O'Sullivan
Scoil Ursula, Blackrock, Cork
In memory of my loving dad Denis

I have a dream to see him again
His smiling face and his tan brown skin
He had a heart of gold
At least that's what I've been told
I believe it because I know
Even though I was only three when he died
My dad was the best man in the world
I miss you Dad
I wish you were here
Even if it was for just one more year.

When I Was Two

Tomas Skelly
Condra N.S., Co. Longford

My father died
When I was two
It was a very sad time for me
I was confused
Because I was two
I didn't understand
And now I'm nine
I understand that I was sad.

Lovehearts by Shannen Kearney

The Honey Bee

Elizabeth Murphy
Scoil Ursula, Strandhill Rd. Sligo

The Honey Bee such a wonderful bug does so
Very much for us
But what do we do for the Honey Bee we
Smash it on the windshield of a bus
The Honey Bee brings us fruit and honey and
The flowers that lighten our lives
All we do in return is take that honey and
Ruin their beautiful hives
The Honey Bee is sometimes a pest and is a
Nuisance if inside our homes
But all it is doing is protecting its babies that
Are nestled inside of its comb
The Honey Bee buzzes and flies and its sting is
Truly annoying I see
But all that I want is to pitifully ask to
Appreciate this wonderful bee

What Am I?

Faiza Raja
Scoil Ursula, Strandhill Rd. Sligo

I'm a dreamer by nature
I'm a risk taker and
Dare to push boundaries
I love life and enjoy every
Moment of living it.
What am I?

Grasshopper by Sarah Fox

Dinner!

Eavan McLoughlin
Scoil Ursula, Strandhill Rd. Sligo

I woke up suddenly in the day,
And thought about what I'd done yesterday…
Nothing fun, nothing great, so I thought,
Today I'll eat someone's mate.
I swam up close near enough to the beach,
But sadly the people were out of my reach!
I really wanted to exercise my gnashers,
And cook up some of my human rashers.

All of a sudden! A human was screaming
And instantly my smile was beaming!
I swam along the beaches shore, excited
To see what treat was in store.

To my delight a human being, spluttering
And splashing and definitely screaming!

I readied my teeth and opened my jaws,
And lunged into my meal, alive and
Raw!

Kun Olin Nuori

Aino Peltola
Aarnivalkea School, Espoo, Finland

Kun olin pieni,
tai pienempi kuin nyt,
ei aalloilla kulkenut tieni,
mutt´ pelko se on hävinnyt.
Kun olin nuori,
tai nuorempi kuin nyt,
oli käsissäni laivan ja ruori,
mutt´ matka se on mennyt.
Vielä olen nuori,
mutta vanhempi kuin ennen,
ja on kädessäni muistojen simpukankuori.
Avaan sen tullen mennen.

Pizza by Alison Devin

129

The Wedding From Hell

Alice Walsh
Rockboro Primary School, Cork

The Horse gave a whinny
The men gave a shout,
The cart gave a clatter,
The bridesmaid fell out.

The horse galloped on,
The cart gave a bump,
It made the bride scream,
It made the groom jump.

Then the horse stopped,
The two fled in a hurry,
A big gust of wind
And the screen went all blurry.

The bride's dress was wet,
She was soaking with cold,
She turned to the cart horse
and gave him a scold.

'You mangy old horse,
Oh, how you make me frown',
He lifted his tail
And the bride's dress was brown.

They ran to the church
The choir began to sing.
The groom then remembered
where was the ring?!!!

He ran to his car
Fantastic no gas,
He felt in his pocket
The ring's there at last.

The wedding would start?
The chances, well, zero
Their three year old son
'Superman' was hero.

He knocked his mum over
The candle went swoosh
The priest was on fire,
The water came whoosh.

Poor priest was soaking
He asked them to leave,
the groom's mouth fell open,
He just could not believe.

The letters were sent
'Bring cards, throw confetti'
But I guess I heard wrong,
Because they all threw spaghetti.

They scolded their son
Oh, no, their worst fears,
He threw back his head
And he burst into tears.

They covered their ears,
Oh the future was bleak.
Oh well, sighed the bride,
We'll try next week.

Clown by Róisín Mannion

London

Lisa Crowe
Brierfield NS, Co. Galway

London is one of the busiest places
With people from lots of different races
There are lots of different sights to see
But London's Eye was the best for me.

In Buckingham Palace, lives the Queen
The biggest mansion, I've ever seen.
The tube is the quickest way to get around.
It's kinda cool being underground!

Big Ben, London Bridge and Trafalgar Square
Are the main attractions over there.
Lots of shops and things to do.
It's my favourite city I've never been to.

See Westminster Abbey on a double decker bus
And a walk in Hyde Park is a definite must.
Get a boat ride on the River Thames.
There's no other city quite the same.

Eurochild by Michael Browne

Stronger

Gary M.Grimes
Scoil Naomh Eanna, Co. Sligo

Sticks and stones
Can break my bones
But a nasty message
On the telephone
Can go much further through you
Past the bone and past the marrow
The road to the heart is twisted and narrow.

But because you chose to fight and bicker
It has only made my skin thicker
And after all you put me through
It would make sense to despise you
But after it all, I need to thank you
Because you made me that much stronger

Cut-Throat War For Popularity

David O'Sullivan
Scoil Naomh Eanna, Co. Sligo

All school bullies can be so nasty,
Making the victim's heart beat faster and faster
They terrorise the child day after day
In the cut-throat war for popularity.

Slowly the child's self-esteem erodes away
As the bully's amusement grows
But even though he thinks he is great
He is ruining the life of a helpless target.

The bully's act of anger was only a façade
Hiding the reality of the problems he had
His separated parents and his alcoholic father
Are destroying him for everyday thereafter.

The onlookers stare at the helpless target
At the fear that resides in his eyes
Trying to avert their gaze
Not knowing what to do but ignore
But evil will only prevail if good men do nothing
In this cut-throat war for popularity.

Gran

Aoife O'Sullivan
Scoil Ursula, Blackrock, Cork

Jumper knitter
Cake baker
Baby sitter
Dinner maker
Great gardener
Good walker
Bingo player
T.V watcher

Gossipers

Stephen Kerins
Scoil Naomh Eanna, Co. Sligo

There are gossipers sitting everywhere
Opening their ears just so they'll hear.
Talking about how he did this and they did that,
Gossiping away like a selfish twat.
So when you're talking look about,
For those nasty gossipers lurking about.
Just so you know, gossiping is a sin
All those gossipers are just trying to fit in.
If you stay a normal person and stay with your friends,
They will help you through the bends.

Hi my name is Scareanna

Alien by Clíodhna Horgan

Goodbye To St. Enda's

John Neary
Scoil Naomh Eanna, Co. Sligo

I started here at the age of four
My mother walked me to the door
Inside the corridor there was yellow and white
Happy and cheerful and always bright.

Into the classroom two by two
We just stood there not knowing what to do
Teacher was smiling when she greeted us
She led us through without a fuss.

Through sport and fun we learned a lot
And a great education we all got
To lead us through our later years
She led us through life without any fears.

Eight years later, it's time to go
From this lovely school in Carraroe
Many friends who are so great
Now some of us must separate

And leaving school I will be sad
But the memories I have are not so bad.

Fall Out!

Sarah Munnelly
Bangor Erris N.S.,Ballina, Co. Mayo

Our dad built us a tree house.
It was really like no other.
We played there many happy hours till
I
Fell
Out
With
My
Brother.

Lion by Rebecca Lally

On That Terrible Day

Sadbh Brennan
Scoil Ursula, Strandhill Rd. Sligo

On that terrible day
Millions of lives faded away
The whole city shook with fear
Nobody realised change was so near

On that terrible day
They crumbled to the ground and there they lay
The whole world stood completley still
The sound of screaming was so loud and shrill

On that terrible day
September 11th as they say
So many loved ones it did take away
On that terrible day

Aš Be Galo

Akvile Anikėnaitė
Vilniaus Martyno Mažvydo,
vidurinė mokykla, Lithuania

Mano dantys kaip kapliai
Ausys–vario pimigai,
O pilkvukas it peliukas,
It nedorėlis dykiukas.

Mano kojos kaip ridikai
–ridinėjas dykai dykai.
Aš dryžuota kaip apuokas.
Aš–be galo nuostabi !

Horse and Paddock by Rachel Ní Sheaghdha

135

The Beach

Michaela Doran
Bangor Erris N.S.,Ballina, Co. Mayo

I like to go to the beach
It is not far out of reach
I like to swim in the sea
As you can clearly see.

The sea is home to many creatures
Some swim high and some swim low
Some have tails and some have feelers
The sea is home to many weird creatures.

I like to walk along the beach
With the sand tickling my feet
I like to twirl and dance
In a walking trance.

I like to picnic on the beach.
And gather shells within my reach.
Full of sand and creepy crawlies too.
I wish you could be here too.

The Rainforest

Bismah Hamid
Scoil Ursula, Strandhill Rd. Sligo

The rainforest such a beautiful place with
Flowers blooming and the birds singing
Through the day
The trees swaying in a light
Breeze high up in the sky while the sun hiding
Its brightness and saying goodbye.
The water falling and steaming quickly by as the
Bees buzz into their yellow, honey hives.
Now the moon is out and the night is here
It's like a glitter shine is everywhere.
The rainforest is such an elegant place if you
Look closely you will see the treasures it stores away.
I'm nearly at the end of my poem.
So now I must say please
Protect our rainforest and it will
Continue to be like this day.

Sunshine by Leanne Finn

A Postman

Frances Hennigan
Kilteevan N.S., Roscommon

He is Autumn
On a rainy day
He is a stamp on a parcel
In a little van
He is a blue shirt
And a green letterbox
He is a drink of tea
And a packet of crisps.

A Farmer

Jamie Granahan
Kilteevan N.S., Roscommon

He is the Spring
On a warm cloudy day
He is a smoking pipe
In a sheep filled field
He is a worn farmers cap
In a tractor seat
He is a cold glass of whiskey
And a plate of spuds.

Speedboat by Conor Booth

Shooting Star

Michelle Kenna
Scoil Naomh Eanna, Co. Sligo

I once wished on a shooting star
I wished that I could have a car
Then on my birthday I got out of bed
But all I had was a sore head.

The Falling Star

Rebecca Mooney
Kilteevan N.S., Roscommon

One night I saw a falling star,
As I was going to bed
It really was an amazing sight
For it flew right over my head.

I ran outside and picked it up,
But one of its points was broken
I bandaged it up very carefully
And then it flew up before I had spoken.

That night I was so very sad
For that little star was fine
But that night I saw a very big star,
I knew that one was mine.

Walking in the Rain by Eilish Murray

Calling Life Out There

Aishling O'Rourke
St. Caillins N.S. Fenagh

Calling life out there, so very far away
Do you feel, do you taste, what games do you play?
Life on earth is brilliant, even when you're feeling blue,
Because you'll have lots of friends around who are
All caring for you.

Do you know of any aliens, is it always night or day?
Do you have a car to get around, is there a month of may?
Is there any nature, what are your friends names?
Did you ever see a fire, did something burst into flames.

I'd love to come and see you I really, really do,
I'd love to see how you live as I don't have a clue.

Alien by Róisín Mannion

Drachen

Jonas Adler
Ernst-Reuter-Schule, Germany

Rot
Das Feuer
Da sind Drachen
Sie sind sehr gefährlich
Rot

Where The Day Rests Longer

Dearbháil Clarke
Stonepark N.S., Co Longford

Where the day rests longer
Is when they all know
When the day rest longer
Then it's time to go

The feeling of pure
Surrender and peace
Happiness and freedom
On a new lease.

Where the day rests longer
I remember her well
We're never alone
That I can tell

We See You Down There

Sherron McGough
St. Caillins N.S. Fenagh

We see you down there
Big and unique
We see you down there
Filled with war and destruction
We see you down there
Polluting the Earth
We see you down there
Hoping not up here

Flowers by Kelly Dorney

Poem

Emilia Zagrian
School Nr 4, Romania

Kevin and Nicky and Me by Nicky Cachia

Ma ridic din tarana.
In jur miroase a tristete.
Patrund cu usurinta in rutina lumii
Apasatoare
Si constat ca viata are gust amar,
Ca soarele este un punct minim de contrast.
Traiesc in cugetul ce-mi strapunge vibratia corporala,
Suflarea-mi e blocata
De iluzia emotiei in care cladesc
Ziduri de sentimente si trairi.
Timpul imi fura fraudulos libertatea,
Imi invadeaza subtil fiinta,
Facandu-ma roaba propriului sistem.
Pamantul este ingropat de pasi,
Iar cerul se dizolva intr-o nuanta de cerneala.
… Raman aici, prezenta, devotata deznodamantului
Care, cu certitudine, va fi atroce.

The Mirror's Story

Erin Whewell
Kilteevan N.S., Roscommon

As it gazes around the room,
Upon the wall it looms
It sees everything passing by
The lets out a mournful sigh
Oh how I wish I could hop and jump
Silent watching gives me the hump
I watch and learn yet never partake
Free me please for pity's sake
I long to enjoy the world
To roam the fields oh now I yearn
To be free is it too much to ask?
But I've got to watch for tis my task!

My Mum Is...

Stacey Ahern
Scoil Ursula, Blackrock, Cork

A life giver
A clothes shopper
A room cleaner
A dish washer
A food cooker
A private taxi
A good listener
My mum is my best friend

J'ai Porté

Arthur Enguehard
Ecole Fellonneau, Nantes, France

J'ai porté une épée de cristal argenté
J'ai porté dix boeufs enchaînés
J'ai porté la terre tout au long de l'été
J'ai porté un sanglier jusqu'à l'entrée de la forêt
J'ai porté un grand chêne arraché
J'ai porté une voiture cabossée
J'ai porté un gros lion affamé
J'ai porté un terrain de football encore tout piétiné.

Gazelle by Sophie O'Callaghan

142

Down A Pathway

Dara O'Mahony
Stonepark N.S., Co Longford

Down a pathway
Deep in the forest
Into the woods
Where do I belong
Searching for happiness
Searching for connection
Where do I belong?
Then I realize
There's no need to grieve
You'll always be
Standing near to me.

The Tree

Thomas Nathaniel Everett
Coomhola N.S., Bantry, Co. Cork

There was in a forest a tree
For more than a century
Its leaves bright and green
For miles to be seen
Till an axe cut it down finally!

Bike by Michael Flanagan

The Words That Blow Away

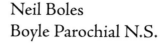

The Poem Refuses

Aisling Creighton
Stonepark N.S., Co Longford

Neil Boles
Boyle Parochial N.S.

The words that blow away
I must reach out and catch
But to find the words inside
I must look in my heart
The words that blow away
Can sometimes be hard to find
But to seek the music in my soul
Finding the poetry in the tune.

The words that blow away
Are right in front of us
But finding the meaning in the words
Is finding the meaning in my heart

The words that blow away
Might be hard to find.
But when I actually catch them
I feel a slight bit of enlightment.

The poem refuses to be written
I'm trying my very best
The words are just not coming
I really don't know why?

The poem refuses to be written
Because it's trying to sleep
It was out late last night
Listening to the piano.

Is there any inspiration
With all these paintings near
Where is my poem?
Oh look it's here

Butterflies by Faiza Raja

To Always Live On A Farm

Aine McLoughlin
Scoil Bhride, Glen, Edgeworthstown, Co. Longford

I want to always live on a farm,
Where everything is calm.
I'd spend all night and day with my animals.
Telling them all my secrets,
I know they won't tell anyone
Silent, Calm everything is right on a farm.

I want to always live a farm
I understand all the hard work
The smells, the noises, the creatures
Late nights and early mornings.
In my wellies all the time.

Mare and Foal by Jennifer Hall

With A Rod In My Hand

Jason Doran
Scoil Bhride, Glen, Edgeworthstown,
Co. Longford

With a rod in my hand
I stroll down to the river
Thinking of the fish in my head
Nothing will stop me
When the hook goes in the water.

Michelle

Molly Brennan
Stonepark N.S., Co Longford

Michelle we miss you and you really cared.
Now were so sad now that you're not there,
I remember the good times and bad
I remember the happy and the sad.
You were as bright as a rainbow after a storm,
In you we found a friend caring and warm.
At my birthday you were there,
Now you're gone we weep and despair.
But now I know you're safe with God.
I remember you dearly forever more.

Unicorn by Rebecca Lally

When They Talk About Angels In Books

Caitriona Mc Tiernan
Stonepark N.S., Co Longford

When they talk about angels in books,
They are probably beside us,
Flying in the air,
Shimmering as they pass the sun,
They must have great fun.
I wonder, maybe they fill the air,
With happiness and prayer,
I wonder what they do right now,
Are they up in heaven?
Or on a cloud?

The Year Goes Off

Kyle Bracken
Collinstown N.S., Co. Westmeath

The year goes off up high in the sky
The fireworks take the year as we say goodbye
The darkness is lit up as we count down
The new year is coming and the old is gone

The year goes off up high in the sky
Old people are gone and new children come.
The sky looks down and sees
The angry wind blowing the rough sea.

I'll Make Music

Maria Henry
Collinstown N.S., Co. Westmeath

I'll make music as the New Year comes
My hands take to the keys.
Waiting for new sounds.
To the music I'll listen
As it twinkles and glistens.
All the new songs for the New Year
All the new songs I'm going to hear
I love to play my piano
Making all the music flow.

Twinkling Star

Lorna Grushinan
Lenamore N.S., Legan, Co. Longford

Twinkling star, shining star
Dancing up above so far
Your sparkle so powerful and so bright
To light up the cold winter night.

You're like a diamond so tiny and small
Sometimes we can barely see you at all
Who ever thought that something so little
Could be so strong and yet so brittle.

A star is such an important thing
It helped the Wise Men find the King
It guides the traveller near and far
Such power it has the tiny star.

The next time you look into the night sky
Be sure to keep a watchful eye
For if you look a way up far
You're sure to see that twinkling star.

Trees by Síofra Ní Mhairtín

I Am The Magic

Niamh O'Meara
St.Mels N.S., Ardach, Co. Longford

In the night
I flow gently
I fly through windows
And shine through stories
Making children happy
I glean through clouds
And rise with the sun.
I am the centre of stories.
Writing the beginning and the end.

In A Split That Can't Be Seen

Sarah Hanley
Scoil Bhride, Glen, Edgeworthstown,
Co. Longford

People carry feelings and sometimes
They feel like running away
From their thoughts and minds.
Inside all people have feelings
On one side good and the other sad.
Sometimes I'm black
And sometimes yellow and happy.
But I never know.
And that for me is a
Split that can't be seen

The Blackboard

Katie Flood
Lenamore N.S., Legan, Co. Longford

We have a mere five blackboards in Lenamore N.S.
But times are moving on, to touch-screens no less.
But as they are forgotten, and forgotten they shall get
Think of all the students and the teachers they have met.
Think of the hardest spelling, or even the longest poem,
Think of what they learn, even when you're gone home,
Think of how smart they get and how lonely they must be,
Over the summer holidays with no one for company.
No one to write on them,
No one to point at them,
No one to comfort them at all,
So the next time you rush by one in the hall,
Just......
Think......

Kim by Louise Kenny

If There Were Two Of Me

Clare Gettings
Aughnagarron N.S.

If there were two of me
I would do twice a much
One of me could go to school
And the other can put her feet up.

Autumn

Laura Woods
Scoil Mhuire Gan Smal, Ballymote, Co. Sligo

She sneaks in quietly
Floating, sweeping away the summer
She plucks the leaves from the trees, creates chills in the air
Finally she disappears making way for winter

Flowers by Emilie Legrand

Summer

Molly Finn
Scoil Mhuire Gan Smal, Ballymote, Co. Sligo

She gallops in happily
Gliding and trotting with no worries
Leaping across fences and prancing in rivers
Scurrying away from the
Wonderful season

When I Score

Fergal Tieran
Collinstown N.S., Co. Westmeath

When I score
There's a feeling
I can't pronounce
When I score in
Basketball I let
My fingers loosen out.
When the ball goes
Through the hoop
I feel happiness
Running through my
Life. But I can't put
My finger on when things
Pass through my life

The Hurling Match

Micheal Daly, Collinstown N.S.,
Co. Westmeath

The clash of the ash
Where hurley smash and
Bones are bashed and broken.

The ref only gives a card
When he plays rough and hard
They say he wont be giving the ref
A Christmas card.

When the player goes training
It is still bucketing raining
Even though he never loses heart.

It doesn't matter if you live in Kerry
Or up in Co. Down
Every county's Dream
It's to win the All Ireland crown.

Football Match by Michael Rafferty

In The Morning

May O'Meara
Condra N.S., Co. Longford

In the morning
I open the day
Shine my light
All over the world.

Nature And Me

Eóghan McManus
Condra N.S., Co. Longford

When I take myself outside
I talk to the air and the sea
I talk to all the animals
Like the birds who live in the trees.

I talk to nature
I talk to rain
I talk to forests
And fields filled with grain.

And one day when I was alone
Nature answered me
She said I am the rain the sun and the sea
And then I understood nature is everywhere in me.

Duck and Bullrushes by Maryanne Hegarty

153

Street Drifters

Noel Sheehy
S.N. Rae na Scrine, Rosscarbery, Co. Cork

The sound of music
From the speakers in the back
Booming like a loud dog's bark
The sound of tyres burning
Around the corner
People move back.
The crowds cheer as the driver
Changes gear and worries
About the rear

The sound of people as they cheer
Drivers pull to the finish line, shifting down a gear.

Pig

Vincent Whitehead
Scoil Mhuire Gan Smal
Ballymote, Co. Sligo

What did we ever do to you?
We just roll around in 'Goo'
Although our rear ends are
Tasty and tender,
Please don't end our life of
Splendour.
In the butcher's window are
We
While our family cry
Wew-wee
But I say please go away.
Become a vegetarian today.

Racing Car by Cathal O'Dowd

Dreaming Wasn't On My List

Maggie-Mai Smith
Aughnagarron N.S.

The list was ok so long
But dreaming wasn't on it
I know where I went wrong

The day it happened
I was so busy
Doing the house work
Feeling tired and dizzy.

After a while I feel asleep
And started dreaming
About dancing sheep...

A Book Of Dreams

Shannon Murray
Aughnagarron N.S.

I opened a book
And out popped a dream
The dream I had been having
the night before
That I'd blanked out of my memory
But had tried to remember

I opened a book
And out popped a dream
A dream of the future
That was yet to come
I flicked the page
To find out what's next.

Fairy by Michelle Higgins

Death Of The Dragon

Lochlann Unger
S.N. Rae na Scrine, Rosscarbery, Co. Cork

Scaly and scarce
Shiny and smooth

The fantasy dragon
Is on the move

Within the cave
There's a princess to save

But who is the knight
That is worthy to fight?

He will travel far east
To slay the clawed beast

He will have to be brave
To enter the cave

The dragon will await
His very own fate

When the knight steps in
With his armour made of tin

The dragon sees the knight
And he knows he must fight

So the dragon blasts fire
To kill the king's sire

As the fire draws near
The knight throws his spear

The spear sails through the air
As the dragon's nostrils flare

It hits the dragon's head
And the dragon is now dead.

Witch by Jason O'Donoghue

Midnight Dancer

Maeve Quinlan
S.N. Rae na Scrine, Rosscarbery, Co. Cork

The stars in her eyes
Shone like the ones in the sky,
She danced with the grace of a willow tree,
Light as the breeze, she twirled so free,
Her hair spun around,
Her feet seemed not to touch the ground,
She glided,
And all decided,
She had the brightest gleam,
They thought she was but a dream.

She had a frock of gold,
Radiant, ragged and bold,
Twists of crimson silk,
Velvet the colour of milk.
Taffeta ruffles around her waist,
The sleeves and the edging is laced,
With chiffon roses, and her shoes,
Are decorated in fiery hues,
She'd learnt the dance, she was no chancer,
Now she disappears,
The midnight dancer...

Dog by Louise Egan

Madraí

Niamh de Buitiméir
Gaelscoil Bheanntraí, Cork

Madra món madra beag
Madra donn madra dubh
Madra mhaith madra dána
Madra chun madra glónach.
Gach sort madra i mo thigh
agus tá gach ceann deas.

I Love Bacon And Cabbage

Shona Cox
Collinstown N.S., Co. Westmeath

I love bacon and cabbage
The way I smell it
When I come in the door
Ready on the table for me
When I get home.

The way it bubbles
Like a dream in my head.
Potatoes with bacon and cabbage
I love them for dinner.

Thanks mom for my
Favourite meal of the day.
I love bacon and cabbage
Mom can I have bacon
And cabbage for dinner tomorrow again?

Il Sole

Maria Giovanna Longo
Scuola Media 'E. Gianturco', Italy
Il sole ci dà luce
e la terra riscalda.
Il sole è vita
e la notte eterna
dilegua.

Chef by Hannah Sheehan

The Memory of the Mountain

Clodagh McEntegart
Dalystown N.S., Co Westmeath

The memory of the mountain
Is stuck inside a stone
of people who went up
and never came home.

And The Stars Are Falling Down

Colm Lowry
Ardnagrath N.S., Co. Westmeath

The stars are falling down
Now the world is doomed
Everyone will be burned alive
and I'm only eleven years old.

If I hide in my bomb shelter
I might survive
I'll be the only one left
And everything will be free.

I'll be the king of the world
I'll be in charge of everything
And the best is
I'll get my electricity for free.

Cat and Mouse by Kevin Duggan

The Light

Ross Gavin
Dalystown N.S., Co Westmeath

I can't see clearly
my body aches and pains
A chill goes through my body
freezing all my veins
Grasping the rails firmly
I hold in my last breath
The light has come upon me
My journey has been set.

A Dagger Pierced my Heart

Evan Quinn
Dalystown N.S., Co Westmeath

A dagger pierced my heart
Pop goes my soul
Up to heaven goes my soul
It was rejected
Satan wasn't there
He was away
Hitler let me in
He tied me to a pole
over some burning coal

For many years I was left there.

Car by Diarmaid Collins

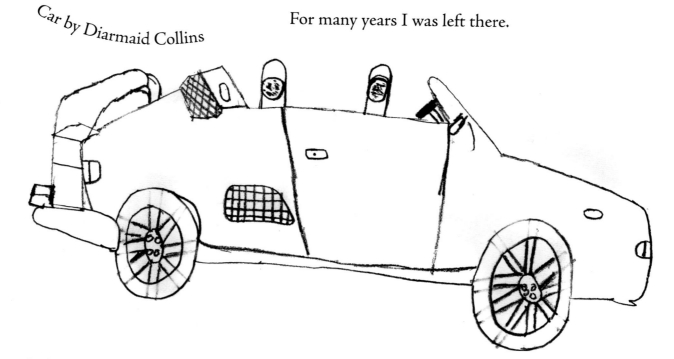

Fire

Callum Muldoon
Scoil Mhuire Gan Smal, Ballymote, Co. Sligo

Fire is a deathly monster
Robs you of your things
Trashes your house.
Takes away your loved ones.

Fire

Sean Hurley
Scoil Mhuire Gan Smal, Ballymote, Co. Sligo

He tears across the room
Destroys the carpet
Rips down the curtain
And kills everyone

Star Wars by Caolán Mooney

Seven Ages of Man

Frédérique Van Loo
Rockboro Primary School, Cork

Baby Bleeding, being born,
Baby crying, mother sighing, trying to make him still.

Schoolchild wanting sweets to fill her tummy,
Trying to look sad at his loving mummy.

Teenager grumpy, calling her friends,
Wanting to be free, trying to make her mum see.

Student working to become a vet,
Listening carefully to get work into her head.

Career is next, looking for clients to come,
Wanting to cure animals and pets.

They marry today, the couple in love,
Giving each other rings with beautiful doves.

The end is sad, she forgets about life,
She's buried under the oak tree and carries a new life.

Tweety by Katie McMorrow

Autumn

Máire Daly
Scoil Mhuire Gan Smal,
Ballymote, Co. Sligo

Autumn is a thief
Strips the leaves off the trees,
Robs you of your outdoor games
Puts the animals to sleep
And takes away the Summer weather.

Global Warming

Niamh Jackson
Presentation Primary School, Dunmanway, Co. Cork

Global warming will come soon,
It will effect the sun, the earth and even the moon,
No to litter,
No to pollution,
They can't be the only solution,
Waves in the sea will get higher and higher,
The sun in the sky will cause forest fires,
Day in and day out smoke is flying in the air,
Look around no one seems to care,
So lets all get together to help the environment,
And everyone can enjoy a happy retirement.

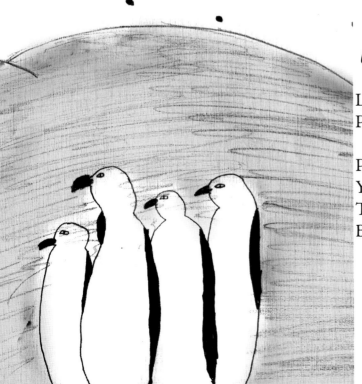

A Penguin Poem

Lauren O'Donovan
Presentation Primary School, Dunmanway, Co. Cork

Penguins are cute, penguins are funny,
You won't find a penguin where it's warm and sunny.
They live in the south where it's covered in snow,
But not in the north with Santa Ho! Ho! Ho!

Penguins by Kelly Byrne

The Unusual Man

Elaine Murphy
Presentation Primary School,
Dunmanway, Co. Cork

An unusual man
came in today,
He was very old
and his hair was grey.

He had yellow trousers
and blue shoes,
It was very funny
we were quite amused.

He said a few poems
We had a good laugh,
Even the teacher did
and all the staff.

Celebrities

Niamh Hill
Presentation Primary School,
Dunmanway, Co. Cork

Celebrities are weird
scary and strange,
Like Britney with no hair
What a dramatic change.

With paparazzi
fashion and shoes,
With mansions,
poodles and pools too!

Well that's my opinion
I'm sure you have one too!
I try to ignore celebrities,
Because they haven't a clue.

The Simpsons by Keith Golden

Lintu

Rosa Niemonen
Aarnivalkean koulu, Espoo, Finland.

Syksyllä se lähtee
Keväällä se palaa
Kun se palaa
Metsä hohkaa kauneuttaan
Metsänväki pitää juhliaan
Mutta karhun vatsa jää kurnimaan

Playtime by Amy Higgins

Drawing A Dream

Shannon Murray
Aughnagarron N.S.

I drew a dream
Plucked from my heart
I sketched it last night.
When I was finished my work.
Pictures running through my head.
Wondering which one to draw.

I drew a dream
Smelling like the flowers.
Sitting on the windowsill.
Coloured brightly
In a summer's morning
Hot and sunny
I drew a dream.

A Baby's Life

Emma O'Sullivan
Christ King Girls School, Turners Cross,
Cork

Babies make a lot of mess
I think you might have made that guess,
Some of them are always shouting
And some are always pouting.

They can be noisy, happy too,
Let's take a look from a baby's view
'I leave surprises in my nappy,
Mammy never seems to be happy'.

My teddy is so cute and cuddly
I take him everywhere,
I don't like to be on my own
Especially when teddy's not there.

Squirrel by Eilish Murray

Bunt

Matti Behnke
Grundschule an der Bake, Mönkeberg

Die Blumen
Sie blühen auf
Bunte Farben leuchten hell
Schön!

Moving House

Shanice Martin
Christ King Girls School
Turners Cross, Cork

The day I moved house
I cried and cried
I lost my neighbour who gave me sweets.
I lost my cousin.
I lost my swing.
I lost my slide.

Now I am in my new house
It's better than I thought
I found new friends
We ride on our bikes
and have lots of fun.
Now that's my poem
So now I'm done.

House by Eilish Murray

I Caught a Cloud

Stephanie Moran
Ardnagrath N.S., Co. Westmeath

I caught a cloud
and put it in my pocket
I brought it home
and put it in a silver locket.
I took good care of it
so it didn't disappear
One day I let it go
back into the sky
to make some rain.

A New Life

Salma Kahmar
Christ King Girls School,
Turners Cross, Cork

I'm Scared.
Everyone is different.
I hear strange voices
I see pale skin
I'm nervous
They stand and join their hands in prayer
Why is everybody looking at me?
I'm frightened
Nobody will play with me
I miss my friends back home

I'm happy
They let me play at lunchtime
I'm good at chasing.

Varsha the Indian Princess

Varsha Koniki
Christ King Girls School, Turners Cross,
Cork

My name is Varsha
I come from India
lovely, sunny India.

I like spicy things to eat
I like spicy smells
My mom makes samosas
at the weekends
Our family eats them all.

My clothes are all different colours
pink, blue, violet and orange.
They sparkle when I look at them
My earrings sparkle too.
My hair is long and black
I wear it in a plait.
My home is a castle on a hill with
flowers all around.

House by Madeleine Carton

There's a...

Sam O'Connell
Scoil Naomh Michael,
Upper Glanmire, Co Cork

There's a ghost
in the house
and its looking at you
Boo
    Boo
        Boo

There's a shadow
on the wall and its following
you
Boo
    Boo
        Boo

There's a spider
in the hall
and its creeping up on you
Boo
    Boo
        Boo

Halloween

Laura O'Sullivan
Scoil Ursula, Blackrock, Cork

Halloween is finally here.
Get on your costumes
Get on your masks
Lets all go trick or treating for the laugh
Eating sweets, watching scary movies all night long
Bats high in the sky
Spiders crawling on the floor
Pumpkins sitting on the walls
Halloween is here so don't forget to say

BOO!!

There's a pumpkin glowing in the dark
and its flickering at you
Boo
    Boo
        Boo

There's a cry outside

Happy Halloween!

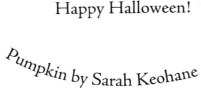

Pumpkin by Sarah Keohane

Faoin Tuatha

Síofra Ní Mhairtín
Gaelscoil Bheanntraí, Cork

Amuigh faoin tuatha
Bím ag gáire
le glondar croí
Ha Ha, hí, hí
Na crainn comh hard
Is na héin sa spéir
Ba mhaith liom bheith
Amuigh faoin aer.

Cuilín Gleoite

Seán MacCarthaigh
Gaelscoil Bheanntraí, Cork

Táim ann!
Ag súil amach leis an bhforeann
Táim ann Páirc an Chrócaigh
Shéid sé an feadóg agus caith sé
isteach an liathrioid
Thainig an liathrioid chughamsa
mó sheans
Rith mé ar nós na gaoithe
Bhí said ar mo dheis agus ar mo chlé
Brostaigh Brostaigh
duirt mé liom féin
Cuilín gleoite
Dhursigh mé.

Tennis Match by Jessica Jane Murphy

My Garden

Cáit Máire Ní Mhurán,
Gaelscoil Bheanntraí, Cork

In my garden there is a trampoline,
three swings and a tall tree.
This tree I like to climb,
I play on it half the time .
Underneath the green grass grows,
Up the top the wind blows.
I usually play in my garden
when the sky is blue,
but when it is raining
were not aloud to.

Untitled

Rose Andersen
Copenhagen Int. School, Denmark

Jeg går og spiser et æble
Fra mit æble træ
Der falder mange blade
Orange, rød, mørkegrøn, gul også brune.

Flowers by Mélani

When I Grow Up

Niamh Daly
Gaelscoil de h'Íde, Co. Cork

When I grow up a teacher I'll be
teaching all the children their ABCs,
I'll do music, painting and songs with them too
I just can't wait there will be so much to do.

Of course I'll do P.E with them,
To help them keep fit and healthy,
We would play basketball hockey and football,
That's just a few of many.

Before I'll be a teacher,
There's still so much to do,
And while I'm getting on with my life,
I'll always know what I'm going to do.

Zip It by Alison Vickery

ZIP IT!

'You'll Always Be My Friend, You Know Too Much'

Fiona McGuckien
St. Patricks GNS, Gardiners Hill, Cork

Friends are like family as such,
'you'll always be my friend, you know too much'
Friends care for each other, each and every day,
Come what may!
Friends are like family as such,
'you'll always be my friend, you know too much'.

172

Raining Cats and Dogs

Lisa Crowley
Presentation Primary School, Dunmanway, Co. Cork

Last night it started raining but all that I could hear
was barks, meows, bangs and bumps coming from above.
But when I awoke next morning the barks and meows,
bumps and bangs all had disappeared.
So when I went outside there was no rain or snow,
But there were heaps of cats and dogs everywhere.

On Top of the World

Charley Morris
Whitehall N.S., Co Westmeath

I'm on top of the world
and fun is holding my hand
Making me happy
Making me laugh
Even sometimes it makes me cry.
On top of the world seeing clouds
Seeing shooting stars
fills me with joy,
On top of the world just having fun.

Shepherd and Sheep by Ciara Dolphin

It's So Much Fun

Joes Genuis
Stella Maris College, Gzira, Malta

It was now break time
The bell started ringing
My friends and I
All started singing
It's so much fun
Going for an outing
Sometimes it's scary
And we start shouting
When I stay quiet
And the children start speaking
We hear some mice
Laughing and squeaking
Outside the school
We hear men walking
Then women come
And we hear them talking

A Beautiful Chaos

Mary Deegan
Dalystown N.S., Co Westmeath

A beautiful chaos is like the
face of the water flowing into the
turquoise lake,
through gods plough down the mountain,
stopping to see a prayer sight,
So precious,
the gorgeous glacier surrounding a hanging
bridge covered in a shawl of snow,
everything together like life's eternal flow.

House by Eva Devaney

A Slimy Gross Snail

Kurt Abela
Stella Maris College, Gzira, Malta

A slimy gross snail, which gets out in the rain
A small slow mollusc which leaves a trail behind
A wriggly camouflage slug which eats greens
Two eyes on top of antennae, which hides under stones
He gets out in the rain and stick to the wall
A pest for farmers and disgusting I must say
It's got a special patterned shell and they are very common to find
A lot of people like to eat them so it is easy for it to end up on a toothpick!

I See An Albatross

Sam Hoiles
Stella Maris College, Gzira, Malta

I see an albatross
It's chewing some pieces of a cuttlefish
It's moving around proudly
It's silvery white with black on its wing
It looks like a snake when it's on the ground
It's featherless
It squeaks to the prey it's about to catch
It's looking for more food
I hope to see another one
Such a magical sight!

Snail by Anthony Ryan

175

Bedtime

Ellen Ní Dhrisceoil
Gaelscoil de H'Íde, Co. Cork

All it is is parents shouting
kids arguing and pouting
walking of in a mood
not getting any food
just getting sent straight upstairs
without another word said.

They just get cross
you get in a fight because
They won't let you keep on a light
'Just two minutes' you plead
But no they won't even let you read.

They switch off the light
and say goodnight
they tell you to go to sleep
but you just say no until they go
But when they are gone out of sight
You climb out of bed and switch back on the ligl

I Have A Dream

Lisa Lyons
Castleplunkett N.S., Co. Rosscommon

I have a dream to do something
big, huge and interesting,
I have a dream that I can't reach
Because I am not like some that
have great big brains and super minds,
So I can't reach the dream I have,
The dream I wish I could reach.

In the Park by Paula Hernández Romero

My Glamorous Granny

Rebecca Mooney
Kilteevan NS, Co. Rosscommon

I have a glamorous granny
She thinks she is sixteen
She even goes to discos,
and she dresses like you've never seen.

For she never wears those granny clothes
But mini skirts and tights
And when she got ready for the ball
She gave my mum a fright.

She never knits and sews
Oh God! No Way! No Never!
But one good thing about her is,
She's the coolest granny ever.

Rock Star by Laura Woods

Nana Mac

Lilli MacMonagle
Crab Lane N.S. Ballintemple, Cork

My Granny is old
Many a story she has told
Like when she was young
She could touch her nose with her tongue.
We all sit down and listen
As all our eyes glisten
At the funny tales she tells.

17

Cherry

Denys Twiss
South School, Abbeyleix, Co Laois

My granny was kind, helpful and loving.
She loved her grandchildren and family
Cherry was her name

She loved me snuggling her
She said I was the best snuggler
Cherry was her name
She was always helpful and wanted to share her hand
and defiantly spoiled me with sweets to best the band!
Cherry was her name

Even through she's gone
She still lives on in my heart
My granny Cherry who was always so happy and merry.

Clown by Thomas Carton

A Locket

Catherine Carthy
Lenamore N.S., Legan, Co. Longford

A locket is nothing to some people
But it is to me.
It is dearly treasured and loved,
My granny gave it to me.
She passed away a few years ago
But she is still here beside me.
I was only two or three.
I miss her soft touch
And the way she makes her tea.
I didn't really know her
But my dad said she was special.
My mum, dad and I visit her grave every Sunday
I tell her everything
So she can catch up on all the scandal.

My Two Little Kittens

Laura O'Driscoll
Gaelscoil Bheanntraí, Cork

My two little kittens
are as soft as mittens
and love playing outside
They twirl and they jump
They run and they hide
but at night we bring them inside.
the girl is called Elliot
The boy is called J.D.
Shhhh everybody
They're going to sleep.

Cats by Ciara Hurley

Mnajdra

Nigel Cini
Stella Maris College, Gzira, Malta

Mnajdra historical temples
All tourists come to see
Legends and stories for you to hear
Talking and discussing about its history
Although it's old, it's still built for you to see.

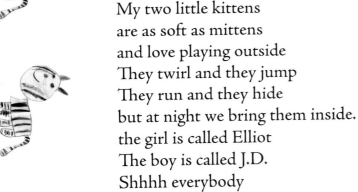

If

Joseph Stanley
South School, Abbeyleix, Co Laois

If I could bring back my granddad I would be the happiest person
in the world.
If I could bring back my dog Lucky I would be delighted
If I could go on holidays all the time I would be a very happy person
If I went to heaven I hope I would meet God and Jesus.
If I had more friends I would be very happy indeed

Flowers by María E. Gómez Cuaresma

My Granddad

Alvin Stanley
South School, Abbeyleix, Co Laois

My Granddad liked to read a lot
He told stories too
With a laugh or two
He was a gentleman
Who was loving, kind, and giving
He worked very hard
on the farm to make a living

Many people say I'm like him
In lots of ways and by the things I do
My granddad died
When I was young
It was a great loss for all
Because he cared for family, friends and neighbours
He always used to call
It was a great pity
He never got to see
All of his seven grandchildren
He only saw me.

Revenge

Eugene McGuinness
Scoil Mhuire Gan Smal, Ballymote, Co. Sligo

Revenge ruins you
Drives you to insanity
Robs you of your pride
Beats you to a pulp

Revenge pushes you over
He is chaos in action
He has one mission
To take over your life

Rugby

Malachy Ryan
Scoil Naomh Micheal, Upper Glanmire,
Co Cork

Rugby is fun and very muddy
Especially when you fall in a puddle
You need lots of gear
I keep mine in a shed
If you want to join Rugby
You go right ahead

Star Wars by Cameron Lumsden

181

The Little Box

Callum O'Brien
Melview N.S., Co Longford

It was dark at the time
I was exploring my gran's house
It was way bigger than mine

In one room there was a dusty bed
And some mice
They saw me and quickly fled.

There was a dusty wardrobe
And a silver lock
I found the key, put it in
And saw a little box

A box that made music
When it was open and shut
The little tones went twinkling
Out the window, and into dusk

An Iasc

Paul Hyland
Scoil Naomh Micheal, Upper Glanmire, Co Cork

Chuir mé mo cheann suas I gcomhair cúpla nóimead ón uisce,
sa chúpla nóimead sin chonaic me gach rud
Chonaic me na páistí ag déanamh caisleán
Na tuismitheoiri ag déanamh ne ceapairí
agus na seantuismitheoiri ina suí ar an gcathaoir beag
oh ba mhaith liom dul ar an trá
I gcomhair lá

Fishing by Barry Loftus

Darker Than Dark

Rachel Kaye Mellor
Zion Parish Primary School, Rathgar, Dublin

I am lonely sitting out here in the darker than dark wood
There is a dusty road that no cars have driven on in years
All I can hear is the continuous sound of the old crow

The cloudy dull sky keeps looking down on me
Ready to burst and come pouring down on me
The mist is starting to come its covering my eyes so I cannot see

All I can do now is feel, I feel the wet grass touching my fingers tips
I have night mares and I cry in my sleep
Day by day I get hungrier and I am getting lonelier

I know now that I am dying, it's easy to tell
I am glad I am going; I have no reason to live any more
I am going up there now into those dull clouds

Now I know why they keep looking down at me

Alone

Conor Prendergast
Zion Parish Primary School,
Rathgar, Dublin

Far away from
anywhere all alone
at night

Ghost costume
hands out

on a country road.

Alien by Robert Quinn

183

He's Up The Road

Lily Roubians
Moyvore N.S., Co. Westmeath

He's up the road waiting
I hear him barking in school
Does he remember me?
Does he do anything when I'm gone?
Or does he just walk all day
Waiting for me to come home?

Dogs by Ella O'Dowd

My Little Sister

Danielle Tormey
South School, Abeyleix, Co Laois

She is a little demon
The way she pulls my hair
She watches Horrid Henry
And like him she can turn into a bear

She has a dimple in each cheek
When she grins and smiles
And when I take her for walks
I have to walk for miles

She is nearly crawling
And whenever I mind her
She always rolls from her tummy to her back
And she's teething
Think of that

Lighthouse

ndrew Jones
ion Parish Primary School, Rathgar,
ublin

p the stony beach
he waves are big
hey hit the rocks
is cold there, very cold
o boat has ever gone there and
me back
t a lighthouse is there
obody knows why
obody lives there any more
t the light still goes on

Ice Stars

Niamh Hebblethwaite
Zion Parish Primary School, Rathgar, Dublin

Winter falling softly upon Autumn's last eve
and from the higher skies
Falling deeply as was ever
Delicate ice stars fall

With a welcome from the earth
so warm and kind

And a goodbye from the clouds
So old and hoarse
Saying that you'll die peacefully
on that beautiful earth

And so the ice stars will fall slowly and gently
Down on winters first dawn

Will peacefully, those ice stars
Rest, sleep and finally die

Fishing by Roísín Laaeen

Ode To Flowers

Chloe Rowland
Grianach House School, Merlin Park, Galway

You came to me when I was born
You were with my Mother when she said I do
You were placed on my Grandfather's grave
You were always there in my life
so now I give you my greatest thanks
Thank you

Galloping Horses by Ella O'Dowd

Garden

Evan Brady
Grianach House School, Merlin Park, Galway

Good place to play
After school I like to
relax on the grass
Day dreaming to myself
Endlessly to myself until
Nighttime

Kitchen Chaos

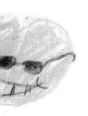

Kayleigh Luby
St. Patricks GNS, Gardiners Hill, Cork

There's chaos in the kitchen
Oh what a state I'm in
My lovely roast potatoes
Have wound up in the bin
The saucepan all boiled over
There's gravy everywhere
If one more thing just happens
I don't think I'll really care.

My Sister's Hair in the Morning

Emily Hughes
St Josephs N.S., Rathwire, Co Westmeath

Frizzled bush
Greece mop
Wet dogs fur
Curly disaster
Bushy mess
Crows nest
Ratty cloth
Brown bomb shell

Going to Play in the Snow

Ian Leavy
St Etchens NS, Kinnegad, Co Westmeath

Wellies and overalls—I'm ready to go
Out in the frost and the thick white snow
I will build a snowman 100 feet tall
So I will reach Mount Everest and see it all
I will see Wales, Scotland and Ireland too
And animals that don't even live in the zoo

I will make snowballs play with my friends and the
leftovers
I'll throw at any target I can
I love throwing snowballs making snowmen
Building snow castles, creating a den!
So each time it snows, I'm ready to play
hat, scarf and gloves—I'm on my way

Reindeer by Lauren Tobin

oh oh

My Granddad

Emma Wallace
Scoil Naomh Micheal
Upper Glanmire, Co Cork

My granddad was a lovely person
He always was my friend.
He was kind and he was cool and always looking out for me,
in the end he was my greatest friend
and now he's gone from me.

Rabbit by Nikola Hanasz

Kesä

Julia Falck
Aarnivalkean koulu, Espoo, Finland

Aurinkoinen kesä
On kuin lämmin linnun pesä
Ja kukat kukkii kukkiaan
Lumet sulaa päältä maan
Kun siilit kömpii pesistään
Nurmi peittää sulan maan
Ja madot kaivaa tunneleitaan.

End of an Era

Eoin Sorohan
Fermoyle N.S., Co Longford

On a cool Summer's morning
Our village fell silent
as we witnessed the final demolition
of a town's forty year landmark

The thundering explosives
Packed against the building erupted
as the startled birds dashed away to safety
the amazing onlookers
Observed the falling concrete

As a cloud of dust descended over the scene
the memories of past workers went with it
Village folk's emotions flooded across their faces
the chimneys would never be set alight again

Each one delivered his farewell
to an old friend
as a new station takes over
so comes the end of an era.

Dolphin by Brigid Borbely

190

School

Jamie O'Donohue
Fermoyle NS, Co Longford

School is the worst
Playstation comes first

Maths and homework and all things bad
sometimes I think I will go mad

Fractions decimals and percentages too
I really don't know what to do

We only like art and P.E.
Sometimes I want to run and scream yippee

That's the way my anger wells
I love it when I hear the bells

Writing

Rebecca Care
Bangor-Erris N.S., Ballina, Co Mayo

I love writing poems and stories galore
and when I stop I want to write more

I'll be outside on good days I'll run and play
But on bad days I'm writing away

When my pen runs out of ink
I'll stop for a moment and then I think

So I'll take out a pencil that's what I said
I'll draw a picture with a scratch of my head

My mum doesn't think I am a saint
but then she changes her mind when I'm covered in paint

She would say 'in the shower' and come out clean
And when you come out you will sparkle and sheen

And when I come out I will be bright
But I'll be covered in paint by the end of the night

Haiku

Michael Browne
Grianach House School, Galway

Haiku comes from Japan
Some people mix the order
of the syllables

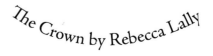

The Crown by Rebecca Lally

191

Leathan Mór Court

Matthew Leneghan
Bangor-Erris NS, Ballina, Co Mayo

My homeland is Ballycroy
but it's a big bog land
I moved to Bangor Erris
My estate is Leathan Mór Court
and it's owned by a big fat man

There are eight houses in it
One is owned by a fisherman who looks like Santa Claus
I don't know where it got its name
But I do know it's the best
Not just in the west
Not just in Ireland
But in the world

Rainbow by Eilish Murray

Anielski Obłok

Jurek Tarnowski
Zespól Szkół, Gdansk, Poland

Ludzie, patrzcie,
co za obłok!
Pod jego spojrzeniem pryska lęk,
ulega mu cały Kosmos,
czuwa nad nami noc i dzień!
Gotów nas unieść aż do nieba,
jego skrzydła są pod ręką tuż, tuż,
poratuje nas w potrzebie
dzielny anioł stróż!

School What made you?

Charlene O' Sullivan
Bangor-Erris N.S., Ballina, Co Mayo

School started when you were young
Playschool was so much fun
Everyday you would play
Until there was that special day

The school was big you missed your Mum and Dad
When you went home you were glad
You thought school was boring, you didn't need to go
That goes to show you didn't know
Every year got harder, you had so much homework to do
You wanted to stay at home and play the PS2

Then there was a bigger school, which you thought first was really cool
You started to choose what you were going to be
It was probably different when you were younger you see

Now you're an adult and have a job, this is the end no need to pretend
This is what you do, this is you
It's the school that made you

Bajka o kotku marzycielu

Maja Tarnowska
Zespól Szkół, Gdansk, Poland

Siedział kotek przy drabinie
myśląc czy wspiąć się czy tez nie
myślał jedną godzinę
myślał długo bo i godzinę drugą
w końcu podjął decyzję
i wspiął się na samą górę
wyciągnął łapkę by pogłaskać chmurę
przekonany że fruwa nad głową
niziutko
a tu licho coraz wyżej ją niesie
więc wspiął się na pazurki
iii...zleciał na sam dół
bez błękitnej chmurki
zamiast w miękkiej upaść trawce
wylądował w pszczół pułapce.
Tuż obok piesek stał
który słysząc smutne miauuuu
złośliwie pomyślał sobie
„nie pomogę nic nie zrobię
bo ten kot na moje oko
łapką sięgał zbyt wysoko"

Wolf by Kevin Farrell

Syksy

Peppi Väänänen
Aarnivalkean koulu Espoo, Finland

On pilvistä ja sataa
Löytyy kuivaa vain puun takaa
Lentävät lehdet
Niitä katsella saa

Huonolla säällä
Sadetakki päällä
On tylsää
Kun ei ole ystävää
Mutta kesällä niitä saa
Joten malta odottaa

Vähän aikaa

Pilna Kasia

Bernard Kiedrowicz
Zespól Szkół, Gdansk, Poland

Jechała Kasia do szkoły na ósmą,
korki i korki, czekała na próżno.
I nagle huk, i nagle brzdęk,
jeden reflektor ze strachu pękł,
lakier się w jakiejś pomarszczył toyocie,
ford wylądowal tuż przy wielkim płocie,
a w mercedesie zgrzytnęły opony,
volkswagen fiata stuknął obrażony...
Na jezdni zgiełk, wielkie zamieszanie,
krzyczą kierowcy, płaczą piękne panie,
a naszej Kasi myśl po głowie krąży,
że dziś do szkoły na pewno nie zdąży.
Przyjechał lekarz w białym ambulansie
i do szpitala pragnie zabrać Kasię,
by ją opukać, prześwietlić co nieco.

Dziewczynce z oczu łzy jak grochy lecą
bo dziś z przyrody miał być temat nowy.
Na noszach leży już pirat drogowy...
Harmider powstał na całej ulicy,
dla naszej Kasi, pilnej uczennicy,
chociaż nie każdy zrozumieć potrafi,
jest najważniejszą lekcja geografii.
Pędzi po schodach, do swej klasy wpada
i dzisiaj pierwsza w ławce swej zasiada.
Lecz dlaczego sala pusta, choć dawno minęła ósma?
—Ty, Kasiu—rzekł dozorca, jak zwykle wesoły—
nawet w niedzielę nie potrafisz żyć bez naszej szkoły.

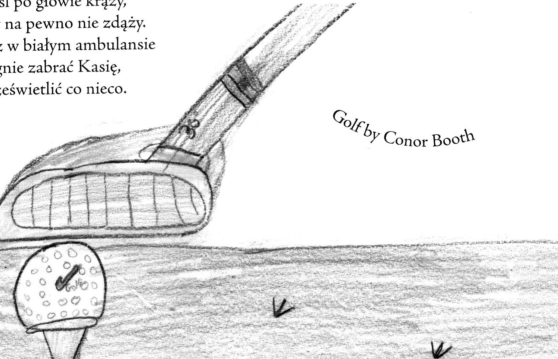

Golf by Conor Booth

Sen

Ola Szczęch
Zespól Szkół, Gdansk, Poland

Ze zdziwieniem się rozglądam...
Gdzie ja jestem?
Powiedżcie, gdzie?
Widzę słodycze, wszędzie słodycze!
Kosze landrynek, pudła lizaków,
zapachy krówek i czekolady,
przepyszne lody, gumy i żelki...
i nagle ... koniec!
Co jest z lodami? Co z czekoladą, no i z żelkami?
Gdzie są słodycze? Gdzie ich zapachy?
Gdzie?
-   Wstawaj, śniadanie!
    Za oknem dzień!
Ach, to był tylko mój słodki sen...

Cows by Juliette Hennessy

Mama

Magdalena Welz
Zespól Szkół, Gdansk, Poland

Jej głos jak śpiew ptaka,
jej oczy jak niebo,
włosy miękkie niczym len,
a w ramionach beztrosko
bezpiecznie można modlić się
aby ta chwila trwała wieczność
nie trzeba myśleć wiele kto to
to mama
drodzy przyjaciele.

Wiersz o tym, jak bardzo nie lubię pisać wierszy

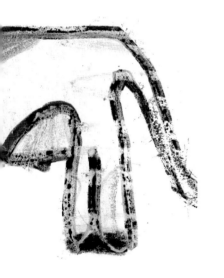

Jagoda Piechocka
Zespól Szkół, Gdansk, Poland

Strasznie nie lubię pisać wierszy,
ale napiszę swój wierszyk pierwszy.
Pani Bożena tak bardzo dusi,
nie ma wyboru
i każdy uczeń wiersz stworzyć musi.
Może napiszę wierszyk o kotku,
który zginął w środku miasta?
Może o myszce, co się utopiła w łyżce wody?
A może o rybce, która malowała na szybce witraże?
Wierszyk na środę ma być gotowy,
a mnie do głowy nic nie przychodzi.
Mam nadzieję, że moje rymy zadowolą panią
Bożenę
i ocenę dobrą otrzymam.
  - Pani Bożeno, proszę gorąco
    ocenę celującą!
    Jeżeli nie, to za karę
    napiszę jeszcze wierszyków parę!

Wierszyk wiosenny

Mateusz Tarłowski
Zespól Szkół, Gdansk, Poland

Kiedy wstaje rano i słońce świeci,
za moim oknem biegają dzieci,
ptaszki ćwierkają, drzewa pączkują,
artyści piszą albo malują,
chłopcy dla dziewzcyn kwiatki zrywają,
tata i mama się uśmiechają,
każdy ma w oczach tyle miłości,
ile w zielonej wiośnie radości.

Tata-marynarz

Piotr Dąbrowski
Zespól Szkół, Gdansk, Poland

Czas nam się dłuży
Brakuje podróży
W domu nuda
Nic się nie uda
A wszystkiemu winien tata
Skończył urlop
I gdzieś lata
Po szerokiej wodzie
I po wielkim świecie
W domu tęskni za nim
Mama z trójką dzieci
Tata pływa
Jeździ wraca
No bo taka jego praca
Jaki piękny czas
Kiedy jest wśród nas
Wymyśla zabawy
Przyrządza frykasy
W wesołym miasteczku
Nie oszczędza kasy
Na statku pływa tata kochany
A gdy go nie ma
My snujemy wakacyjne plany.

Winged Horse by Shauna Farrell

Dreams

Mahnoor Ali
Grinach House School, Merlin Park, Galway

Once you close your eyes,
You fall asleep
So now its time to go to the land
of dreams
You can swim with a dolphin in the ocean sea
Or go on a surfboard
Nearly seems like you're free
if you want something more exciting you could be king of the world
or be very famous and sing.

That's what could happen in the land of dreams
until you wake up in the morning

Dog by Siobhán Hurley

Dreams

Ivana Vrućinić
Children's Cultural Center Belgrade, Srbija

Dreams are as beautiful as flowers
Dreams help you to grow wings
And fly off somewhere new.
You travel, visit different wolrds
Land in meadows and on lovely flowers.
Dreams don't last long
Just long enough to be beautiful,
Then Mummy wakes you to go to school
And everything seems a bit strange

Mój wiersz

Radek Krawczykiewicz
Zespól Szkół, Gdansk, Poland

–„Napisać wiersz"
kto wpadł na taki głupi pomysł?
pytam ja, dyslektyk, dysortograf Radomir.
Nie potrafię i nie mam weny
więc znowu lufę dostanę
od pani Bożeny.
Gumkuję kreślę i tak wciąż od nowa
boli mnie ręka i boli mnie głowa.
Szukam natchnienia u mamy i bratra,
lecz mama w kuchyni
bratr u jakiejś panny...
może mi tata pomoże,
gdy wróci z pracy?
Lecz gdy mój tata z pracy wraca,
wtedy do niego przychodi praca...
Przeziągam się nad zeszytem leniwie
i myśle,
jak się usprawiedliwię.
Chyba się rzucę przez okno...
ale na dworze dziś mokro...
Już wiem!
Wyznam prosto i szczerze,
skąd brak talentu się bierze:
Przecież z Krawczykiewicza nikt nie zrobi
Mickiewicza!

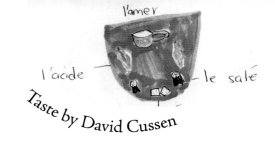

Taste by David Cussen

Co to je?

Kateřina Berková
Gymnázium Jiřího Ortena,
Kutná Hora, Czech Republic

Všichni víme, co to je...

Je to zvíře,
někdy k nevíře.

Má to dlouhé čtyři nohy,
pozor, nemá to parohy!

Má to ale bystré uši,
slyší kolem jít každou duši.

Krásná očka,
jak ta kočka.
Tělíčko má vypracované,
budete do něho zamilované.

Všichni víme, co to je?
pejsek, co nedá pokoje! ☺

Já škola a kamarádi

Daniel Jehlička
Gymnázium Jiřího Ortena,
Kutná Hora, Czech Republic

Škola

Jana Kružíková
Gymnázium Jiřího Ortena,
Kutná Hora, Czech Republic

Škola to je učení,
občas také mučení,
někdy je to zábavné,
jindy ale vůbec ne.

Při fyzice hokus pokus,
učitelka kouká na kus
ohořelé hmoty,
kape jí na boty.

O hodině hudebky
zatroubíme na trubky,
zazpíváme písničku,
zapíšeme notičku.

Při výtvarné výchově
malujeme na chodbě,
jsme šikovní malíři,
kteří štětcem na zeď míří.

Škola, že by nepřítel,
Ne, to není.
Přece kamarádi,
ti to změní.

Karel, Franta, Martin, Jan...
s těmi přece nejsi sám.

Ve škole se potkáme,
vtípky si tam předáme
a učení si zopáknem.

Škola to jsou informace,
zábava a poučení.
To jsou moje velké cíle
vzdálené na celé míle.

Kamarádi napořád,
poučeni navždy.
Dodržujte školní řád,
ať nás má pan školník rád.

Škola, že by nepřítel,
ne to není.
Škola základ života,
to je oč tu běží.

Funny Face by Vincent Legrand

Váhání

Tereza Frýbortová
Gymnázium Jiřího Ortena, Kutná Hora

Už šest let chodím do školy
doma se dřu s úkoly.

Špatně vstávám, těžká záda,
těším se, že najdu kamaráda...

Pak je den jak sluníčko,
těšíme, ne maličko.

Na písemky, na zkoušení???
Tohle zatím problém není.

Na lavice, na židle? Tabuli a křídu?
Kdepak! Uvidím zas svoji třídu.

Je tu plno prima lidí,
ta pohoda se hned vidí.

A tak než být v posteli,
raději půjdu do školy.

Škola

Jakub Kersch
Gymnázium Jiřího Ortena, Kutná Hora

Do Školy, jak je v Čechách známo,
se nechodí večer, nýbrž ráno.

Chodějí tam holky, kluci.
Malí. velcí, tlustí, tencí.

Učení je nebaví,
však občas se i pobaví.

O víkendu mají volno.
Na zábavu, na blbosti–při kterých si zlámou kosti,
a pak zase povinnosti.

Kromě vědomostí z toho nemají nic,
jen míň volna a fakt nic víc.

Není ti však nadarmo, a navíc je to zadarmo!!!

Balloons by Emily Hall

Occupation.....Peace

Ossama Mohammed
Palestinian Child Arts Center, Palestine

What should we do, under occupation…
We can't let it stop our life,
Stop us from doing our daily work
Stop our dreams…
We should study, play, sleep, eat, to become better people
But war, occupation, destroyed all our dreams
Even they did not allow us to think of peace…
We need to live in peace…
We are children, the same like all the children of the world

Flowers by Katelyn Scanlon

Hope For Peace

Suha Zenat
Palestinian Child Arts Center, Palestine

People were dreaming of peace
But now, we are dreaming of peace
And to end the occupation in Palestine
We still have HOPE…
HOPE for new future
For Peace
For freedom
For dignity
We want to live
We will not lose the hope…

Peace, pace, salam, paix, paz.........

Sahar Abdeen
Palestinian Child Arts Center, Palestine

Always they told us,
That we start the peace process in Palestine...
But TV shows us different things,
The children killed, the trees died, the houses destroyed,
The tanks walking in the streets...
PEACE is just small word but it means a lot...
It gives us the purpose to live,
Make our dreams real
Always we hope that one day our dreams will come true
We still have the hope
And believe that peace will come one day...
Peace
Salam
Paz
Paix
...

Ponies by Holly Hurley

My Belgrade

Gora Pastuović
Children's Cultural Center Belgrade,
Srbija

In early spring my Belgrade
Wakes up slowly from its dreams.
Gently, gradually, to the song of birds,
Without taking the smile off children's
faces.

But there's nothing like winter–
I'm so proud of white Belgrade.
I'm proud of it in yellow autumn
When the golden leaves are falling.

I like the summer days best
Belgrade glows like a comet.
Then I realize how much it sparkles,
It means so much to me whatever the
season.

Wherever I am dream about it,
And sing this song about it
I sing about the city of my birth.
Belgrade–the best place on earth!

I Hate Being Small

Mihaljo Jovanoćić
Children's Cultural Center Belgrade, Srbija

I hate being small,
When tall pupils pass by me
The desire to grow flows through my veins.

I hate being small,
I'm saying this because I keep expecting
To grow so much
That everyone says
'Hello big boy!'

You're one metre tall,
Peter tells me.
What can I do—
I'll just have to wait
Until I grow
At least one centimetre.

Pinnochio by Nick Varnavsky

Grandpa

Marija Jovanović
Children's Cultural Center Belgrade, Srbija

Yesterday I was wondering
All day long
Why I always
Dream the same dream.

He's holding me on his lap
Calling me his 'doll',
A silk cushion in his hand.
He tells me stories
About himself
And all the proud heroes around him.

My grandpa is modest,
My grandpa is quiet
And other say
That he is quite someone.
My grandpa is a real hero.
Today, once again
I'm thinking about
How fate has stopped him
From holding me, cooing to me,
Waiting for me to go to sleep,
And me from seeing him, knowing him,
Instead of just dreaming about him.

PEACE......NO PEACE??????

Haneen Talal
Palestinian Child Arts Center, Palestine

Every body is waiting.....waiting what???
PEACE???
I don't know what to write about??? peace...war...
I want to laugh...
I want to cry...
I don't know what to do???
I was happy and sad at the same time...
I don't know whether to laugh or cry, this is our life...
Waiting for peace

Don't by Neasa MacHugh

TV And Peace

Deema Sultan
Palestinian Child Arts Center, Palestine

I decided to watch TV,
All the news...2 killed, 3 killed...war...Iraq
Palestine...
There is no place for peace in this world...???
What I can do to help people to live in peace???
I shouted peace, salaam, paz...
Peace and just peace to Palestinian peace
To all the people of the world

I Love Secrets

Butterflies by Ciara Hurley

Anja Marković
Children's Cultural Center Belgrade, Srbija

My cheeks are on fire
Inside me hides a secret.
I carry it with me everywhere
And try to make sure that no one
Knows about it–but in vain.

I have a serious face
With an enigmatic twinkle in my eyes,
But I know that in a moment
My secret will be no more.

Impatiently, as if it just flies out of me,
I tell it and at that moment everything changes.
I'm calm now, with no more worries,
Now my secret has released its charm.

Where Love Blossoms

Nadja Glišić
Children's Cultural Center Belgrade,
Srbija

Love blossoms on the sea coast,
Love blossoms on the hill top,
On the highest mountain
In the deepest valley,
Love blossoms at the end of the world.

Love can blossom everywhere.
On the sea coast,
On the hill top,
On the highest mountain,
In the deepest valley.

But best of all in your heart!

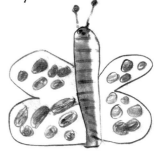

207

A Shower of Laughter

Lena Simić
Children's Cultural Center Belgrade, Srbija

When I laugh, I really laugh,
I don't know why myself.
They say:'She laughs like a drain'.
But what's so bad about that?
Am I supposed to get angry
And worry about it and shut up?
I'm going to laugh very clearly,
Heartily, loudly, deafeningly.
Let them be totally amazed
And cry if they want to,
But with joy not with sadness.
Let the salt tears flow,
Get the umbrellas out!
I'm going to laugh out loud,
And what's so terrible about that,
I really don't know

Roi des Forêts

Gilbert Haberlin
Enfants Francophones De Cork, Gardiners Hill

Mon beau sapin, roi des forêts
Comme j'aime ta parure
Qui brille à Noel, quand tu descends du ciel
Pour faire rêver petits et grands!

Clown by Roman Ignatovsky

I Was Shy

Ognjen Karadžić
Children's Cultural Center Belgrade, Srbija

A long, long time ago I met
A girl with a sweet smile
She was the cure to all my ills
I've never met such a girl since

She had such beautiful hair
She wanted to talk to me
This was the first time I had called a girl with freckles on her nose
A lady.

Spotty Dog by Ciara Hurley

I saw her again the other day
When looking through some photos
With a heavy heart I could but dream
Because it was, you might say, love.

There were certain things I never told her
But I still think about her now
Time passes and memories age
And all I have is a photograph.

I remember we'd listened to the same music,
We'd though of each other
Continually typed messages to each other
For ages and ages!

I never found out
Whether she liked me or not
The reason I never told her
Was because I was shy

I've met other girls
But nobody has loved me like she did,
Perhaps because of my eyes woven with sorrow
Because I've never got over her.

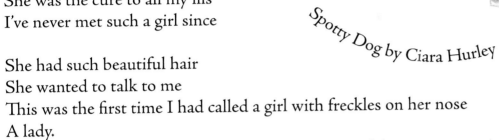

L'arbre à cubes!

Kieran Vélon
Enfants Francophones De Cork, Gardiners Hill

Dans ma chambre pousse un arbre à cubes,
Non! C'est vrai ?
Oui! Et même qu'ils sont attachés aves des tubes !
En été, ils changent de couleur
Verts, jaunes et même bleus quand il pleut !
A Noèl, ils deviennent blancs comme le ciel
Je sais qu'il n'y a que moi qui le voit
Mais peut importe, car c'est mon arbre à moi!

Santa in the Snow by Chloe Nation

Les Animaux

Joséphine Rogers
Enfants Francophones De Cork, Gardiners Hill

J'adore les animaux
Les petits et les gros !
Mes préférés sont les chats et les chiens.
J'ai un peu peur des requins
Car on dit qu'ils sont coquins
A la maison, j'ai un chien
Il mange des bonbons, même quand c'est les miens!
Les animaux, quelle bande de rigolos!

Le Monde Merveilleux Des Pingouins

Luc Galland
Enfants Francophones De Cork
Gardiners Hill

Il est doux et gentil
Il ne ferait jamais de mal
A n'importe quel animal !
Il a parfois peur d'aller dans l'eau
A cause du vilain requin dodo
Son meilleur ami c'est moi
Car je ne veux pas qu'il ait froid !
Un jour, il a eu un bébé
Alors il est parti lui chercher à manger
Depuis je ne l'ai jamais revu
Très malheureux, je suis devenu!

Bugs Bunny by Gemma Golden

Ah! Les fleurs! Quel bonheur!

Emilie LeGrand
Enfants Francophones De Cork, Gardiners Hill

J'aime les fleurs, mais je n'aime pas le beurre !
Cela me brise le coeur quand elles meurent !
Les fleurs peuvent être de toutes les couleurs
Mais celles que je préfère sont les bleues claires
Car elles me rappellent les yeux de ma mère !
J'adore les fleurs rouge et or
Quand le soleil brille, elles luisent comme un trésor
!
Ah ! Les fleurs ! Quel bonheur !

Une Vache

Juliette Hennessy
Enfants Francophones De Cork, Gardiners Hill

Qui a dèja vu une vache qui fait des claquettes ?
Moi j'en ai vu une l'été dernier, elle était vraiment chouette
Elle etait blanche et rose avec un chapeau melon
Et dansait sur le pont d'Avignon ...
Qui a déjà vu un chien jouer de la guitare ?
J'en ai recontré un place de la gare
Il était noir et marron et jouait de l'accordéon ...

Si J'étais Chinoise

Madeleine Carton
Enfants Francophones De Cork, Gardiners Hill

Si j'étais chinoise, je ferais des phrases
Pour dire les merveilles de la vie au soleil
J'écrirais tous les mots qui me passent par la tête
Et cela ressemblerait à une jolie fête
Maintenant, les rayons me brûlent les yeux
C'est beaucoup plus chaud que le feu
Je regarde les papillons voler dans le ciel
C'est très beau et je sens l'odeur du miel
La campagne est belle, inutile d'aller en Chine !

Caterpillar by Ciara Hurley

Pomme

Lily Ségrétier
Enfants Francophones De Cork, Gardiners Hill

Je suis une pomme verte
Assise sur un vase
Au milieu de la table
J'ai peur de tomber
Sur le canapé
Ma peau devient rouge
Si quelqu'un me bouge
Je ne veux pas qu'on me touche
Et surtout pas qu'on me mange !

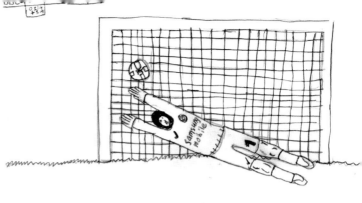

J'adore Sauter

Louise Vélon
Enfants Francophones De Cork, Gardiners Hill

J'ai une corde à sauter
De toutes les couleurs
Quand je saute, c'est un vrai bonheur !
En ville et au parc, elle m'accompagne
J'adore sauter à la corde
Grâce à elle, je prends l'air
Et reste dehors toute la journée!

Score! by James Hannon

Le Ski

Niamh Roussel
Enfants Francophones De Cork, Gardiners Hill

Moi, maman et mon frère avons fait du ski
La montagne était belle et le ciel aussi!
Faisons la course, hop on démarre:
Maman tombe tête la première
Le nez dans la neige et mon frère avec!
Je suis arrivée première, comme j'étais fière!

Butterfly

Akshay Kakamav.
R.V.H.S.S. Chockli, Thalassery, Kannur, Kerala. India

Butterfly butterfly
you come me
flying flying butterfly
play with me
come come fly
flying you flying you
very fastly.

Postman by Cha

Esto Es Libertad

María E. Gómez Cuaresma
C.E.I.P. Juan Ramón Jiménez, Huelva, España

Siempre voy al río,
siempre iré,
veo una flor,
nunca me olvidaré.

Es un bonito lugar
flores, flores, y flores
que siempre cogeré.

Mi casa

Paula Hernández Romero
C.E.I.P. Juan Ramón Jiménez, Huelva,
España

Mi casa tiene una ventana,
por la que cada mañana
me asomo y veo amanecer.

También veo mi calle,
pequeña y estrecha
con sus árboles y flores,
bancos y farolas,
hombres y mujeres
que pasean de la mano.

Dog

Cow

Mon Ballon

Thomas Carton
Enfants Francophones De Cork, Gardiners Hill

Le matin, je me léve et je tape dedans
Dans la cuisine, il file manger ma tartine
Dans la salle de bains, il prend son bain
Mais dans la cour, c'est moi qui court!

A l'école je le lance aux copains
C'est toujours vers moi qu'il revient
Dans la classe, je fais des passes
A la récré, je le mets de côté
Quand l'école est finie, je suis ravi!

Tous les soirs, je m'entraîne
Pour devenir champion du ballon rond
Un jour, je serai comme Zidane
Vainqueur absolu des tirs au but!

L'ogre

Lee Russel
Enfants Francophones De Cork, Gardiners Hill

Monsieur l'ogre est malade
Quatre yeux lui ont poussé
Trois nez l'ont transperçé
Et deux bouches lui sont apparues
Il est allé chez le docteur
Qui lui a dit : Mon Dieu vous me faites peur !
Et à la pharmacie, ils ont beaucoup ri !
Alors il est rentré chez lui et s'est mis vite au lit !

Earth by Aishling O'Rourke

Estoy Solo

Gabriel Moreira Dos Santos
C.E.I.P. Juan Ramón Jiménez, Huelva, España

Estoy solo,
siento una brisa
en el aire,
murmullos, voces...
estoy solo, sin nadie,
sin nada pero nunca me asusto.

Veo algo;
una luz.
Estoy en la
oscuridad,
total iré a
la luz,
allí me siento
seguro,
aquí no.

Me Siento Solo

Yanine Wendez Salvatierra
C.E.I.P. Juan Ramón Jiménez, Huelva, España

Está lloviendo
me siento solo
con mi gato leo
un cuento y me
acuerdo de todo.

Eurochild by Claire Hobbs

Bolivia

Pedro Luis Medina Coca
C.E.I.P. Juan Ramón Jiménez, Huelva,
España

Bolivia es mi país
nunca me olvidaré de ti.

Y mi ciudad Sta. Cruz
siempre tendrá mi amistad.

El Pájaro

Gabrielle Viana de Soussa
C.E.I.P. Juan Ramón Jiménez, Huelva,
España

Vuela un pájaro,
canta en el árbol,
mueve sus alas,
salta de rama en rama,
mira a otro pájaro,
juega con él
y pían de alegría.

Bruce Lee by Nicole Griffin Healy

El jardín

Marta Torres González
C.E.I.P. Juan Ramón Jiménez, Huelva,
España

Yo tengo un jardín
lleno de flores
de varios colores
y muchos olores.

Una se llama jazmín
la que más huele en el jardín
y la que más me gusta a mí.

Un Pajarito

Mélani
C.E.I.P. Juan Ramón Jiménez,
Huelva, España

Desde mi ventana
vi un pajarito
que volaba muy alto.

Le di de comer en mi mano
y todos los días venía.

Nos hicimos amigos
¡Qué lindo el pajarito!

My Desk by Conor Maguire

219

Une Fleur

Sinead Gillain
Enfants Francophones De Cork, Gardiners Hill

Si j'étais une fleur, je serais toujours de bonne humeur
Si j'avais un plan je saurais d'où vient le vent
Si j'étais rigolote, je m'appellerais sans doute Charlotte
Mais j'ai seulement neuf ans, et tout mon temps
Pour refaire le monde à l'envers!

Santa by Bridget Power

Sunny House by Clíodhna Ní Chonchúir

Mona Lisa

Vincent Legrand
Enfants Francophones De Cork,
Gardiners Hill

Mona Lisa me sourit
Elle est si jolie!
Avec ses cheveux noirs, ses lèvres douces
On dirait qu'elle me suit du regard
Leonardo de Vinci l'a peinte en Italie
Mais c'est à Paris qu'on peut l'admirer
Au musée du Louvre, elle a atterri!

Homework

Jemma Coogan
St Columba's G.N.S., Douglas,
Cork

What is Homework?
Homework is something
put on earth
to torture children!

We complain and complain
but there is nothing to
be done. Even when there is
lots of sun.

We get more homework everyday.
I wish it would just go away!!!!

Tractor by Daniel Curley

Index of Poets and Artists

Index of Schools

If you would like to enter a poem or a drawing for

EuroChild 2010

just post it to:

Eurochild 2010
c/o Tigh Filí
50 Popes Quay
Cork
Ireland

or email it to:

info@eurochild.net

Don't forget to include and please print:

Your name, address and age.
The name, address and phone number of your school.
Entry fee of two euros per child (not per entry)

Further details can be found on
www.eurochild.net

The decision of the judges is final and no correspondence can
be entered into.

The Eurochild team gratefully acknowledges the support of our friends!

Brian Crowley MEP
Carmel McCarthy
John Costello
Benny McCabe
Aoife Tierney
Moya Power
PKT